Bracket Battles
The Thrill and Strategy of
Men's March Madness

Introduction

Every spring, a unique kind of frenzy sweeps across the United States. Office workers huddle around water coolers, students fill out online brackets between classes, families cheer on their alma maters, and even those with only a casual interest in college basketball suddenly become analysts overnight. This is the spell of March Madness—a whirlwind of emotion, unpredictability, and strategic brilliance that grips the nation for three unforgettable weeks. At the heart of this chaos lies the bracket: a simple grid that transforms into a battlefield of hopes, heartbreaks, and historic upsets. Bracket Battles: The Thrill and Strategy of Men's March Madness is a deep dive into this cultural and sporting phenomenon, exploring not only the excitement it brings but also the complex layers of strategy, history, and psychology that underpin it.

March Madness is more than a basketball tournament. It's a collective experience, uniting people of all ages, backgrounds, and regions in a shared passion for competition. Whether you're a die-hard fan who memorizes team stats or a first-timer picking winners based on mascots and colors, the bracket gives everyone a stake in the outcome. This sense of inclusivity and unpredictability is what makes the tournament so exhilarating. In no other sport are David-and-Goliath battles so frequent or so consequential. It is the one arena where a 15-seed can rise from obscurity to challenge the giants, capturing national headlines and the hearts of millions.

But while the madness may seem random, there's a method to it. Behind every upset lies a backstory of preparation, coaching, and a strategic edge. From understanding how the NCAA selection committee builds the bracket to identifying trends that signal possible upsets, this book unpacks the tools that experts and enthusiasts alike use to outwit the chaos. You'll discover how advanced analytics, player matchups, team momentum, and historical data all play roles in shaping the tournament's outcome—and your bracket's success.

We'll also celebrate the stories that have made March Madness legendary: buzzer-beaters that echo through time, underdog runs that defy logic, and coaching strategies that shift the tide of games. You'll meet the players and coaches who became household names in the span of a few thrilling nights, and learn how one moment can define a legacy.

Beyond the hardwood, Bracket Battles also explores the cultural explosion surrounding the tournament—from billion-dollar broadcasting deals to the rise of online bracket challenges, from campus watch parties to the economic impact on host cities. It's a phenomenon that transcends sports, touching aspects of business, psychology, media, and American identity.

Whether you're looking to fill out a winning bracket, understand the deeper strategies of the game, or simply relive the magic of past tournaments, this book is your courtside pass. So sharpen your pencils, grab your bracket, and get ready for a journey into the thrill, heartbreak, and glory that is Men's March Madness.

Chapter 1
The Madness Begins

Before the first tip-off, before the buzzer-beaters and bracket busters, before the heartbreak and hysteria, there is a moment—a collective breath held across the nation as fans, analysts, and hopeful underdogs await the madness. It's a moment that has become a ritual, steeped in tradition and adrenaline, as the bracket is revealed and a dream begins. This chapter explores the origins, cultural roots, and the electrifying atmosphere that transforms March into something extraordinary. Welcome to the beginning of the madness.

March Madness, officially known as the NCAA Division I Men's Basketball Tournament, wasn't always the cultural behemoth it is today. It began modestly in 1939 with just eight teams and a single goal: to crown a national champion in collegiate basketball. No billion-dollar TV deals. No office pools. No Cinderella stories captivating the nation. But what it did have was the seed of something powerful—an elimination format that guaranteed high stakes and dramatic outcomes. Over the decades, that seed grew into a phenomenon that now captivates millions.

The term "March Madness" itself wasn't coined by the NCAA. It originated in the 1930s in reference to Illinois high school basketball tournaments and was later adopted by sportscaster Brent Musburger in the 1980s to describe the NCAA Tournament's wild unpredictability. Since then, the name has become synonymous with chaos, emotion, and the beauty of imperfection in competition.

What sets March Madness apart from any other sporting event is its unique ability to blend structure with spontaneity. The single-elimination format means there are no second chances. Every game is win or go home. This do-or-die scenario levels the playing field in a way that few other tournaments do. Powerhouses like Duke, Kentucky, and Kansas enter each year with the weight of expectations, while smaller schools—schools you may never have heard of—see their chance to etch their name into history with just one upset.

But the madness isn't limited to the court. It lives in the living rooms, classrooms, and office break rooms across America. Brackets are filled out with a mix of hope, hunches, and hard data. Debates rage over sleeper picks and Final Four locks. People who don't watch a single regular-season game suddenly care deeply about a school's rebounding average or free throw percentage. For three weeks, the country becomes a nation of bracketologists.

And behind all the excitement is the very real human element. These are student-athletes—some playing for the love of the game, others chasing a shot at professional careers—who lay it all on the line in front of the world. For many, this is the pinnacle of their basketball journey, and they rise to meet the moment with breathtaking passion and resilience.

In this chapter, we will delve into how March Madness came to be, why it matters so deeply to so many, and how it has become one of the most emotionally charged and strategically fascinating sporting events in the world. The madness doesn't just begin with the first game. It begins here—with the history, the heart, and the hype that set the stage for everything to come.

Origins of the NCAA Tournament

The NCAA Tournament, now a cultural juggernaut known as March Madness, had humble beginnings rooted in a time when college basketball was still fighting for its place in the American sports landscape. It began in 1939, a time when radio was the primary medium of mass communication, and the idea of a nationwide college basketball competition was ambitious, if not entirely experimental. That year, just eight teams competed in the first-ever NCAA Men's Division I Basketball Championship. There were no million-dollar sponsorships, no roaring crowds in domed stadiums, and certainly no billion-dollar broadcast rights—just a vision, a hardwood court, and a belief in the game's potential.

The brainchild of the tournament was Harold Olsen, then the head coach of Ohio State University. Olsen saw a gap in the college sports system: while there were conference champions, there was no unified method to crown a national champion in basketball. The National Invitation Tournament (NIT), which began a year earlier in 1938, had already taken the lead, offering a postseason competition that attracted strong teams. However, Olsen's vision differed—he imagined a tournament sponsored and governed by the National Collegiate Athletic Association (NCAA) itself, ensuring credibility, fairness, and broader national interest.

In its inaugural year, the tournament was a modest affair. The games were played in just two locations—Patten Gymnasium at Northwestern University and the California Coliseum in San Francisco. The University of Oregon defeated Ohio State in the championship game, earning the distinction of being the first NCAA basketball champion. Dubbed the "Tall Firs" for their height,

Oregon's team set a precedent for fast-paced, team-oriented play that would become a staple in future tournaments.

Despite its successful launch, the NCAA Tournament struggled to gain traction in its early years. The NIT, hosted in the famed Madison Square Garden, was seen by many as the more prestigious event. It wasn't until the 1950s and 1960s—particularly with the rise of powerhouse programs like Kentucky, UCLA, and Indiana—that the NCAA Tournament began to pull ahead. The turning point came when the NCAA prohibited teams from playing in both the NCAA and NIT tournaments, forcing programs to choose—and ultimately shifting the balance of power.

Television changed everything. By the 1960s and 70s, with increased national coverage, the NCAA Tournament began to enter living rooms across America. The drama of single-elimination play, the rising stars of college basketball, and the unpredictability of every game made it ideal for TV audiences. The 1979 championship game between Magic Johnson's Michigan State and Larry Bird's Indiana State became one of the most-watched basketball games in history, signaling the beginning of a new era.

From its humble eight-team origins to today's 68-team spectacle, the NCAA Tournament has evolved into a national celebration. But at its heart, it remains a competition built on the same principles Harold Olsen envisioned: fair play, fierce competition, and the chance for every team—no matter how big or small—to carve its name into history.

Why March? The Power of Timing

March marks the end of winter and the beginning of spring, a transitional period that aligns with the culmination of the college basketball season. As the cold fades and days become longer, the

NCAA Men's Basketball Tournament begins, offering a renewed sense of excitement. The timing coincides with the end of the regular season and the beginning of conference tournaments, making March a natural climax point for the sport.

The regular season typically runs from early November to late February. By March, teams have either built strong tournament résumés or are fighting for survival in their conference championships. Conference tournaments provide an opportunity for lower-seeded teams to secure automatic bids, while higher-ranked programs aim to confirm their standing. This last-chance setting adds urgency and drama to March, reinforcing its reputation as the most important month in college basketball.

The sports calendar further enhances the significance of March. Following the Super Bowl in early February, there is a brief lull in major American sports. Major League Baseball is still in preseason, the NBA is midway through its regular season, and professional football is in the off-season. This timing leaves March relatively open, giving the NCAA Tournament an unrivaled spotlight. Viewers and media attention focus entirely on the tournament, allowing it to dominate headlines, social media, and national conversation.

The tournament's structure fits seamlessly into March. Beginning with Selection Sunday, the bracket is revealed, followed by three action-packed weeks of competition. The First Four, First and Second Rounds, Sweet 16, Elite Eight, and Final Four occur in succession, each stage intensifying public engagement. The schedule builds suspense and allows audiences to track progress in real time. The natural progression of games throughout March ensures continuous attention and a steadily increasing emotional investment.

Academic calendars also contribute to March's significance. Most universities schedule spring break during this time, enabling student-athletes to travel and compete without conflicting academic obligations. Fans, especially college students, are free to attend games or watch from home without class interruptions. This synchronization enhances participation from schools and student bodies, bolstering the tournament's energy and atmosphere.

March is also when fans engage in bracket culture. Bracket challenges, office pools, and friendly competitions become widespread as people across the country fill out their predictions. This aspect of the tournament is time-sensitive. The release of the bracket in mid-March provides enough time for analysis and speculation, but not so much time that enthusiasm wanes. The compact, high-stakes schedule encourages immediate involvement and rapid emotional investment.

The psychological and cultural atmosphere of March supports the tournament's popularity. The arrival of spring symbolizes change and opportunity. The unpredictability of the tournament, with its underdog victories and dramatic finishes, reflects this seasonal shift. The convergence of sports, culture, timing, and community in March creates the perfect storm for national attention.

March is not merely the setting but the engine of the NCAA Tournament's success. Its placement in the calendar enhances viewership, participation, media coverage, and emotional impact, making the madness both timely and timeless.

The Cultural Impact of Bracket Season

The NCAA Men's Basketball Tournament has evolved from a college sporting event into a national cultural phenomenon, and at the heart of this transformation is the bracket. What began as a way to track matchups has become a symbol of competition, community, and even identity for millions of fans. The bracket season, which kicks off each March with Selection Sunday, extends far beyond basketball—it shapes conversations, creates traditions, and unites diverse groups of people under the shared thrill of prediction and possibility.

One of the most significant cultural impacts of bracket season is its unparalleled ability to foster mass participation. Every March, people across the United States—and increasingly around the world—fill out brackets, often without deep knowledge of the sport. From college students to corporate executives, from lifelong fans to casual observers, the bracket becomes a shared experience that transcends age, gender, and background. Office pools emerge in workplaces, bracket challenges pop up among friends and families, and online contests with multimillion-dollar prizes attract millions of entries. This universal appeal turns March into a collective event, a kind of sports-based holiday season.

The bracket's simplicity is part of its power. Predicting the outcome of 63 games is a straightforward challenge on the surface, but the unpredictable nature of the tournament makes perfection nearly impossible. This paradox draws people in—encouraging friendly rivalries, personal research, and community debates. It also offers a rare kind of interactivity in sports, where fans don't just watch the games but feel personally invested in their outcomes. A last-second three-pointer doesn't just decide who advances—it can make or break a person's bracket, adding an extra layer of intensity to every game.

Media coverage amplifies the cultural reach of bracket season. News outlets, sports networks, and social media platforms devote extensive resources to analyzing matchups, sharing expert predictions, and tracking popular picks. The rise of bracketology as a field of analysis has turned sports journalists and data analysts into mini-celebrities during March. Television broadcasts feature live bracket breakdowns, highlight buzzer-beaters, and follow emerging Cinderella stories, turning everyday teams and players into national sensations overnight.

Social media further intensifies the communal aspect of bracket season. Fans share screenshots of their brackets, celebrate victories, lament early exits, and engage in debates over controversial calls or surprising upsets. Memes, reaction videos, and viral moments become part of the tournament's digital fabric, extending its cultural footprint well beyond the court. Platforms like Twitter, Instagram, and TikTok become extensions of the arena, where real-time reactions and fan creativity flourish.

The bracket has also influenced consumer behavior. Brands run marketing campaigns tied to the madness, and businesses see increased activity, especially in food, drink, and entertainment sectors. Sports bars, restaurants, and streaming platforms experience spikes in engagement during tournament games. Merchandise sales, ticket demand, and travel plans all rise in March, underscoring the bracket's economic impact as well.

Bracket season is more than just a sporting ritual—it's a cultural event that brings people together through shared excitement, competition, and hope. Its influence reaches into homes, offices, classrooms, and digital spaces, making March Madness not just a tournament, but a tradition.

What Makes It "Madness"?

The term "March Madness" captures the chaotic, unpredictable, and emotionally charged nature of the NCAA Men's Basketball Tournament. It is a label that encapsulates the shock of upsets, the thrill of buzzer-beaters, the rise of underdogs, and the collective frenzy that grips fans and players alike. But what truly makes it madness is not just the high level of competition—it's the convergence of pressure, drama, and national attention in a condensed, win-or-go-home format that defies logic and expectations.

At the core of the madness is the single-elimination structure. Unlike professional leagues that use best-of series to determine winners, the NCAA Tournament gives each team only one chance to survive and advance. This structure raises the stakes for every possession, every timeout, and every decision. A bad shooting night, an untimely injury, or a hot-handed opponent can abruptly end a team's season, no matter how dominant they were during the regular season. The sense of urgency this format produces results in games filled with relentless energy, emotional swings, and memorable moments.

The unpredictability of the tournament adds to the madness. Every year, lower-seeded teams defy the odds and defeat traditional powerhouses. A 15-seed beating a 2-seed, a last-second three-pointer from a mid-major school, or a double-overtime thriller between unknown programs can become the defining moment of the entire tournament. These upsets fuel the drama, as the so-called "Cinderella teams" capture the hearts of fans and bring an element of fantasy to the competition. The success of these teams often defies conventional basketball wisdom and statistical models, reminding everyone that anything can happen in March.

The emotional investment from fans, players, and coaches intensifies the madness. For players—many of whom are in their final year of eligibility—this is the culmination of years of dedication, and their last shot at glory on a national stage. For coaches, a single tournament run can define a career or change the trajectory of a program. For fans, particularly alumni and students, the tournament becomes a personal journey, with their identity and pride intertwined with the outcome of each game. This emotional weight contributes to the explosive celebrations and heartbreaking tears that unfold with every victory and defeat.

Media coverage magnifies the madness. From the moment Selection Sunday airs, the tournament dominates headlines, talk shows, and social media. Highlights of game-winning shots, court-storming fans, and last-second miracles are replayed endlessly. Analysts break down every play, fans argue over brackets, and everyone becomes an expert overnight. The sheer volume of games—often played simultaneously across different locations—creates a nonstop viewing experience that overwhelms and excites audiences.

The madness is also reflected in the speed and scale of it all. Over the course of just a few days, dozens of games are played, brackets are destroyed, heroes are born, and stories are written. The momentum never slows, keeping fans glued to their screens from morning until late at night.

What makes it madness is the perfect storm of structure, emotion, unpredictability, and national obsession. It's not just basketball—it's a cultural spectacle where logic is suspended, giants fall, dreams ignite, and the line between victory and defeat is often no more than a single shot.

Chapter 2
Anatomy of a Bracket

Each March, millions of fans across the country stare at the same puzzle: the NCAA Tournament bracket. At first glance, it's just a 68-team grid split into four regions, filled with seed numbers, unfamiliar matchups, and possibilities. But behind its clean lines and symmetrical layout lies a system rich in strategy, history, and calculated decisions. The bracket is more than a visual representation of a tournament—it's the beating heart of March Madness. It determines the path to glory, fuels debates, and turns fans into armchair analysts. Understanding how this bracket is built and how to interpret its nuances is essential to appreciating the tournament's depth.

The bracket is a map of dreams and destruction. It begins with Selection Sunday, the annual unveiling of which 68 teams made the cut and where they are placed. Thirty-two teams earn automatic bids by winning their conference tournaments, while the remaining 36 receive at-large bids based on their performance throughout the season. The selection committee is tasked with one of the most scrutinized responsibilities in sports: deciding who gets in, who gets left out, and how the entire bracket is shaped. These decisions are based on a mixture of metrics, records, rankings, and human judgment.

At the core of the bracket are seedings. Each team is assigned a seed from 1 to 16 in their region, which represents their relative strength compared to other teams in the field. A 1-seed is considered among the best, while a 16-seed is typically a small-conference champion with a lower ranking. Matchups are arranged accordingly, with the highest seeds facing the lowest in the first round. While this system is designed to reward stronger teams with easier paths, the tournament's history is littered with unexpected results, proving that seeds are guidelines—not guarantees.

The bracket is also geographically divided into four regions, usually named after their hosting locations: East, West, South, and Midwest. These regional groupings are designed to minimize travel and maintain a degree of fairness, but they also serve to balance competitiveness across the tournament. The top four overall teams are each given a 1-seed in a separate region, and the rest of the field is distributed to ensure that no region is overloaded with elite teams. Even this process is complex, as the committee must also consider rivalries, potential rematches, and logistical constraints.

For fans, the bracket is a source of both excitement and agony. Filling one out is a ritual—predicting winners round by round, imagining upsets, and choosing a champion. It's a blend of knowledge, superstition, gut feelings, and hope. Some study statistics and past performances; others choose based on mascots or colors. But once the games begin, the bracket becomes something else entirely: a living document of drama, unpredictability, and shattered expectations.

In this chapter, the anatomy of the bracket will be dissected in full. From the structure and selection process to seeding logic and regional strategy, we will explore how this simple chart holds the power to thrill, confuse, and unite millions every spring.

Understanding the Tournament Format

The NCAA Men's Basketball Tournament follows a single-elimination format that features 68 teams competing over a span of three weeks, culminating in the crowning of a national champion. This format is one of the defining features of March Madness, contributing significantly to its unpredictability and excitement. Every game is a high-stakes battle, where one loss ends a team's journey, regardless of their past performance or national ranking. This all-or-nothing structure levels the playing field and makes room for both dominant powerhouses and unexpected underdogs to make deep runs.

The tournament begins with what is known as the "First Four." These are four play-in games involving the lowest-seeded at-large teams and the lowest-seeded automatic qualifiers. The winners of these games advance to complete the traditional 64-team bracket. From that point forward, the tournament proceeds in four main rounds: the First Round (Round of 64), the Second Round (Round of 32), the Sweet 16, and the Elite Eight. These are followed by the Final Four and the National Championship game.

Each round cuts the field in half. In the First Round, 64 teams compete in 32 games. The winners move on to the Second Round, where 32 teams compete in 16 games. The 16 remaining teams then enter the Sweet 16, and those victors proceed to the Elite Eight. The final eight teams are divided into four regional champions, each emerging from their respective region—East, West, South, and Midwest. These regional winners advance to the Final Four, where the national semifinals and final are held at a preselected neutral site, often in a large stadium capable of hosting tens of thousands of fans.

The structure of the bracket is designed to reward higher-seeded teams with theoretically easier paths in the early rounds. For example, a 1-seed will face a 16-seed in the First Round, while a 2-seed will face a 15-seed, and so on. However, upsets are common, and lower-seeded teams often play with nothing to lose, resulting in unpredictable and thrilling outcomes. This unpredictability has given rise to the "Cinderella story" phenomenon, where a low-seeded team makes an unexpected deep run, often knocking off multiple higher-seeded opponents along the way.

Games are played at neutral venues across the country to maintain fairness and avoid giving any team a true home-court advantage. These venues rotate annually, and cities bid for the right to host games. The early rounds are usually played in smaller arenas, while the Final Four and National Championship are held in large stadiums that can accommodate the vast crowds and national media presence.

Another element of the format is its tight scheduling. Teams play multiple games over the span of a few days, testing not only their talent but also their endurance, coaching, and depth. Quick turnarounds between rounds challenge players and staff to prepare efficiently for unfamiliar opponents.

This format, with its simple premise and complex outcomes, is what gives March Madness its enduring appeal. Every possession matters, every mistake is magnified, and every game has the potential to make history.

Seeding: Art, Science, or Politics?

Seeding in the NCAA Men's Basketball Tournament is one of the most debated and scrutinized aspects of March Madness. It is the process by which the 68 qualifying teams are ranked and placed into the tournament bracket. On the surface, it appears to be a straightforward system—assigning numbers from 1 to 16 within each of the four regions to indicate the relative strength of the teams. However, the method behind this ranking is anything but simple. It involves a mixture of statistical analysis, subjective judgment, and strategic considerations. The question persists: is seeding an art, a science, or a form of politics?

The scientific aspect of seeding lies in the use of data and performance metrics. The NCAA selection committee evaluates each team using several tools and statistical models. Key factors include overall win-loss record, strength of schedule, NET rankings (the NCAA Evaluation Tool), and quadrant system performance. The quadrant system categorizes wins and losses based on the quality of the opponent and game location—home, away, or neutral. Teams are also assessed based on head-to-head matchups, road wins, and records against other tournament-bound teams. These objective criteria help ensure that seeding is grounded in performance rather than perception.

However, despite the use of metrics, there is an undeniable art to the process. The committee must consider factors that numbers can't fully capture, such as team momentum, injuries to key players, or the context of certain wins and losses. A team that stumbled early in the season but finished strong might be seen as more dangerous than one that started hot and faded. Likewise, teams with the same record may be seeded differently due to how convincingly they won games or how battle-tested they are against high-caliber opponents. This interpretative side of seeding introduces subjectivity, relying on the committee's basketball judgment and collective experience.

Politics can also play a role, intentionally or not. Despite efforts to maintain neutrality, certain biases can influence decisions. Power conference teams often receive the benefit of the doubt over mid-majors, even when records are similar. The perceived strength of a conference, the historical success of a program, or even media visibility can subtly sway rankings. Additionally, the committee must adhere to guidelines that prevent certain matchups—like early rematches or conference rivals playing in the first two rounds. These rules sometimes result in seeding adjustments that serve bracket integrity over strict merit.

Geography and television appeal may also be taken into account. Higher-seeded teams may be placed closer to home for travel considerations, while marquee programs might be distributed in a way that boosts national interest. These decisions may not be overtly political but can influence outcomes in ways that go beyond the court.

Ultimately, seeding is a complex blend of logic and discretion. While data and analysis provide a foundation, human judgment fills in the gaps, and external pressures subtly shape the outcome. Whether viewed as an art, science, or politics, seeding remains a critical component of March Madness—one that shapes the tournament's narrative, determines potential upsets, and adds yet another layer of intrigue to the most unpredictable event in sports.

Regions and Matchups Explained

The NCAA Men's Basketball Tournament bracket is divided into four regions: East, West, South, and Midwest. These regions are not just geographical labels—they serve as structural frameworks that shape the tournament's progression and determine the matchups that fans follow with intensity each March. Understanding how regions and matchups are constructed provides insight into the strategic balancing act performed by the NCAA selection committee and helps explain why certain paths to the Final Four are more challenging than others.

Each region consists of 16 seeded teams (after the First Four is complete), ranked from 1 to 16 based on overall performance, strength of schedule, quality wins, and other metrics. The highest-seeded team in each region is known as the "No. 1 seed," and each region will contain one of the tournament's top four teams overall. These four No. 1 seeds are placed in different regions to ensure that the top contenders don't meet until the Final Four. The committee also designates one of the No. 1 seeds as the "overall top seed," and that team is placed in the region closest to its home campus.

Matchups within each region are structured to reward higher seeds with supposedly easier paths. In the First Round, the 1-seed plays the 16-seed, the 2-seed plays the 15-seed, and so on, down to the 8-seed vs. 9-seed matchup. These opening games create immediate tension: while higher seeds are favored, upsets are always possible, and lower-seeded teams often bring energy and momentum into these contests. The 8 vs. 9 games are usually the most evenly matched, often decided by slim margins.

As the tournament progresses, winners from each pairing advance within their region. This means that every team must navigate through its assigned regional bracket to reach the Final Four. The structure creates a logical flow—after the First and Second Rounds, each region has four remaining teams (Sweet 16), then two (Elite Eight), and finally one regional champion who earns a spot in the Final Four. This format ensures that all teams, regardless of initial seeding, must win four games against regional opponents before advancing to the national semifinals.

The location of each region's games adds another layer of complexity. While early-round matchups are held at neutral venues, the NCAA attempts to place higher-seeded teams at sites closer to home, especially in the First and Second Rounds. This geographic proximity can offer subtle advantages, such as fan support and reduced travel fatigue. However, as the tournament advances to the Sweet 16 and Elite Eight, games are played in predetermined regional sites, and the advantage of playing near home diminishes.

The committee must also consider conflicts and constraints when creating matchups. Teams from the same conference are generally not placed in the same region unless necessary, and early-round rematches from the regular season are avoided. These rules can influence which teams are shifted from one region to another, affecting both fairness and competitiveness.

The regional structure and strategic pairing of teams create the foundation for the drama and excitement that define March Madness. Every region tells its own story, filled with rivalries, upsets, and the relentless pursuit of a Final Four berth.

Key Dates and Deadlines

The NCAA Men's Basketball Tournament operates on a precise schedule, with key dates and deadlines that dictate the flow of the competition and the planning process for teams, fans, broadcasters, and organizers. These dates are critical to understanding how the tournament unfolds, from the conclusion of the regular season to the crowning of the national champion. Each phase of March Madness is built around these milestones, creating a rhythm that defines the madness itself.

The first significant date is Selection Sunday, typically held on the second Sunday of March. This is when the NCAA Selection

Committee reveals the full 68-team tournament field. Thirty-two teams earn automatic bids by winning their respective conference tournaments, while the remaining 36 at-large bids are determined by the committee based on team performance, rankings, and other criteria. On Selection Sunday, fans across the country tune in to see where their teams are seeded, who they'll face, and what region they've been placed in. It's also when millions of brackets begin to be filled out.

Immediately following Selection Sunday, the First Four kicks off. These are four play-in games involving the four lowest-seeded at-large teams and the four lowest-seeded automatic qualifiers. Played on Tuesday and Wednesday, these games determine which teams fill the final four spots in the main 64-team bracket. The First Four marks the official beginning of tournament play, and its outcomes finalize the structure of the traditional bracket.

Next comes the First Round, typically played on Thursday and Friday following the First Four. This round features 32 games across the four regions, as 64 teams compete in a fast-paced, two-day basketball marathon. These are some of the most intense and exciting days of the tournament, as fans watch multiple games simultaneously, often witnessing surprising upsets and buzzer-beaters.

The Second Round follows immediately on Saturday and Sunday, featuring 16 games as the field is cut in half. Teams that survive the opening weekend advance to the Sweet 16, which takes place the following Thursday and Friday. These games are hosted in regional venues and feature only the top 16 teams, typically representing the strongest and most battle-tested programs in the tournament.

The Elite Eight is played on the subsequent Saturday and Sunday, with four games determining the regional champions. These winners advance to the Final Four, the national semifinals, held one week later on Saturday at a major stadium selected well in advance. The two semifinal winners then meet in the National Championship Game on Monday night, typically the first or second Monday of April, concluding the tournament.

Beyond game dates, other key deadlines include the final submission of team rosters and eligibility paperwork, television broadcast schedules, and ticket releases. Teams also have strict NCAA-mandated schedules for travel, practice sessions, media obligations, and rest periods.

These carefully orchestrated dates ensure that March Madness unfolds smoothly, with each phase building anticipation and intensity. The consistency of the schedule allows fans to plan viewing parties, fill out brackets on time, and follow every twist and turn of one of the most thrilling competitions in all of sports.

Chapter 3
Cinderella Stories and Shattered Dreams

Each year during March Madness, as the nation watches elite programs battle for supremacy, a different narrative quietly captures the collective imagination—one of unexpected heroes, dramatic upsets, and emotional triumphs. This is the story of the Cinderella teams, those underestimated underdogs who defy expectations and turn the bracket upside down. They arrive with little fanfare, often representing small schools from lesser-known conferences, but their performances on the national stage become the stuff of legend. At the same time, the tournament is also a graveyard of dreams for many top-seeded giants whose seasons end in stunning defeat. This chapter explores both sides of the coin: the joy of the Cinderella and the heartbreak of the favorite.

The term "Cinderella" in college basketball refers to a low-seeded team that advances far into the tournament, often defeating multiple higher-seeded opponents along the way. Their success is not just a surprise—it is a disruption of the expected order, a challenge to the status quo of college basketball hierarchy. These teams often feature unknown players, overlooked coaches, and fanbases that rally behind the belief that anything is possible. In the span of just a few days, a team can go from anonymity to national fame, forever etching its name into tournament history.

The magic of Cinderella runs lies in their unpredictability. A buzzer-beater by a 13-seed over a 4-seed, a dominating performance by a mid-major school against a storied powerhouse—these moments capture the spirit of March Madness. They remind fans why the games are played and why seeds, reputations, and rankings mean little once the ball is tipped. These stories transcend the court, symbolizing resilience, belief, and the power of teamwork. They are the moments when preparation meets opportunity, and the entire basketball world takes notice.

But for every Cinderella that rises, there is a titan that falls. Shattered dreams are the other side of March Madness, where top-seeded teams with national title hopes suffer early exits. For these programs, the expectations are enormous, and the pressure is relentless. A single off-night can unravel an entire season of dominance. The emotional toll is visible—players in tears, stunned fans, and coaches facing tough questions. These collapses become part of tournament lore, sometimes overshadowing a team's accomplishments during the regular season.

The contrast between Cinderella stories and shattered dreams is what gives March Madness its emotional depth. One team's victory is another's heartbreak. For fans, it's a rollercoaster of emotions; for players, it's the realization that one game can change everything. The intensity of the stakes, the finality of the losses, and the unexpected triumphs are all magnified in the bracket's unforgiving structure.

This chapter dives into some of the most iconic Cinderella runs in tournament history, the ingredients that make such runs possible, and the psychological and strategic factors that lead to shocking upsets. It also examines the collapse of highly favored teams, the burden of expectations, and how those moments redefine the legacy of players and programs. Together, these stories form the soul of March Madness—where dreams are both made and broken.

The Magic of Underdogs

The allure of March Madness lies in its unpredictability, and nowhere is that more evident than in the rise of the underdog. Every year, teams from smaller conferences or those seeded in the double digits challenge and often defeat college basketball's traditional powerhouses. These teams, known as underdogs, become the heart and soul of the tournament, capturing national attention and inspiring fans across the country. Their journeys embody the essence of competitive spirit, resilience, and belief in the impossible.

Underdogs are often defined by what they lack—resources, national exposure, high-profile recruits—but it is precisely this absence that fuels their magic. These teams enter the tournament with minimal expectations and everything to gain. They play loose, fearless, and with a chip on their shoulders. The lack of external pressure often works in their favor, allowing them to embrace the moment and compete with passion and grit. Opponents, particularly higher-seeded ones, sometimes underestimate them, which can lead to complacency or a slow start—an opening underdogs are quick to exploit.

The structure of the tournament enhances their chances. In a single-elimination format, one great performance can be enough to topple a giant. Unlike professional leagues where teams have to win best-of series, the NCAA Tournament offers no second chances. This creates a volatile environment where effort, momentum, and even luck can play decisive roles. A hot shooting night, a defensive stand, or a timely turnover can swing the game in favor of the team least expected to win.

History is filled with memorable underdog runs that have become legendary. Schools like Florida Gulf Coast, George Mason, Loyola Chicago, and Saint Peter's are etched into March Madness folklore for their improbable journeys through the bracket. These teams didn't just win games—they won the hearts of fans, the respect of analysts, and the attention of the media. Players who were previously unknown suddenly became household names, and coaches earned national acclaim. Their success stories serve as reminders that belief and unity can overcome any odds.

What makes the magic of underdogs so compelling is their ability to create emotional connections. Fans gravitate toward these stories because they reflect broader life themes—overcoming adversity, defying expectations, and proving doubters wrong. For alumni and small-school supporters, these moments are deeply personal. For neutral fans, underdogs provide a chance to cheer for the unexpected and to witness something historic. In a world often dominated by power and prestige, underdogs offer a refreshing narrative of merit, effort, and heart.

Media coverage plays a significant role in amplifying underdog stories. As soon as a lower-seeded team pulls off an upset, their journey becomes headline news. Players are interviewed, highlights are broadcast repeatedly, and their campus communities celebrate in scenes of pure joy. This exposure not only elevates the team but also brings long-term benefits to the program—recruitment improves, donations increase, and the school gains national recognition.

The magic of underdogs is a defining feature of March Madness. It represents the unpredictable nature of competition and the beauty of sport. It proves that, in basketball as in life, the least expected can rise the highest when given the chance.

Legendary Upsets That Shocked the World

March Madness has long been a stage where giants fall and dreams ignite. Among the most unforgettable moments in NCAA Tournament history are the legendary upsets—shocking victories by low-seeded, often overlooked teams over elite programs with championship aspirations. These games don't just alter brackets—they become etched in the cultural memory of college basketball, celebrated for their drama, defiance of odds, and seismic impact on the tournament landscape.

One of the most iconic upsets occurred in 2018, when the University of Maryland, Baltimore County (UMBC) made history by becoming the first No. 16 seed to defeat a No. 1 seed in the men's tournament. Their 74–54 dismantling of the University of Virginia, the tournament's overall top seed, wasn't just an upset—it was a complete domination. Virginia entered the tournament with a reputation for suffocating defense and consistency. Yet UMBC, a small school with little national recognition, played with fearless energy and precision, shocking viewers and rewriting the record books. That single game became a symbol of possibility—proof that no team is invincible.

Another unforgettable upset came in 1985, when Villanova, an 8-seed, defeated powerhouse Georgetown in the national championship game. Georgetown, led by Patrick Ewing and coached by the legendary John Thompson, was heavily favored to win. But Villanova executed one of the most efficient shooting performances in tournament history, hitting 78.6% of their shots and playing near-perfect basketball. The upset was not only unexpected but came on the sport's biggest stage, delivering one of the greatest underdog victories of all time.

The 2006 George Mason Patriots added their own chapter to upset history with a remarkable run to the Final Four as an 11-seed. Along the way, they defeated basketball blue bloods Michigan State, North Carolina, and Connecticut. George Mason's Cinderella story was a testament to teamwork, smart coaching, and belief in the impossible. Their victories inspired mid-major programs across the country, proving that sustained excellence and strategic execution could overcome even the most elite opponents.

Florida Gulf Coast University, dubbed "Dunk City," captured national attention in 2013 with their explosive style of play and fearless attitude. As a 15-seed, they defeated 2-seed Georgetown and 7-seed San Diego State to become the first 15-seed to reach the Sweet 16. Their high-flying dunks, fast-paced offense, and energetic celebrations electrified fans and turned the relatively unknown school into a March Madness sensation.

In 2022, Saint Peter's University added another remarkable upset to tournament lore. As a 15-seed, they stunned 2-seed Kentucky in the First Round and continued their improbable journey all the way to the Elite Eight, defeating Murray State and Purdue along the way. With limited resources and national exposure, Saint Peter's became the lowest seed in history to reach that stage of the tournament, and their fearless play captured hearts nationwide.

These legendary upsets serve as a reminder of the unpredictable beauty of March Madness. They celebrate the underdog spirit, challenge the hierarchy of college basketball, and reinforce why the tournament holds such a special place in American sports. Each upset is more than just a game—it's a story of courage, unity, and the enduring power of belief.

What Fuels a Cinderella Run?

A Cinderella run in the NCAA Men's Basketball Tournament is one of the most captivating storylines in all of sports. When a low-seeded team defies the odds and advances deep into the tournament, it captures the attention of the nation. But these magical runs are not the result of luck alone. Behind every Cinderella story lies a powerful combination of factors—talent, coaching, chemistry, preparation, and a fearless mindset—that together create the perfect storm for an underdog's rise.

One of the most critical elements fueling a Cinderella run is team chemistry. Unlike many high-major programs that rely on one-and-done players destined for the NBA, mid-major schools and lower-seeded teams often feature veteran rosters filled with juniors and seniors who have played together for years. This continuity results in stronger on-court communication, trust, and cohesion. These players know each other's tendencies and strengths intimately, allowing them to function as a unit under pressure when games are tight and stakes are high.

Experienced coaching is another major factor. Cinderella teams are often led by coaches who have spent years developing systems that maximize their players' abilities. These coaches may not have the biggest names or budgets, but they often excel in strategy, in-game adjustments, and motivation. A well-prepared game plan tailored to counter a higher-seeded opponent's weaknesses can be the key to an upset. Moreover, these coaches frequently instill a belief in their players that they belong on the big stage—a belief that can make all the difference.

Playing with nothing to lose is a powerful psychological advantage. Lower-seeded teams enter the tournament with minimal outside expectations. This lack of pressure can lead to fearless play, where athletes take bold shots, push the pace, and challenge traditional powerhouses with confidence. Conversely, higher-seeded teams often carry the weight of national attention, championship hopes, and media scrutiny. This dynamic can result in tighter play, especially if the favorite falls behind early or faces unexpected resistance.

Strong guard play is a common denominator in many Cinderella stories. In high-pressure tournament games, experienced and steady guards help control tempo, limit turnovers, and make crucial plays in the final minutes. A reliable backcourt can slow the game down when needed, hit clutch free throws, and break full-court pressure from more athletic teams. Guards who can dictate pace and handle the ball under duress give underdogs the stability they need to pull off close wins.

Matchup advantages also play a role. A lower-seeded team may have a style of play that specifically disrupts a higher-seeded opponent—such as a stifling zone defense, a sharpshooting offense, or a methodical pace that frustrates faster teams. Additionally, opponents may underestimate the underdog's talent or preparation, leading to defensive lapses or mental errors.

Finally, momentum and belief drive Cinderella runs forward. Winning the first game boosts confidence and creates a sense of destiny. As attention grows and the spotlight intensifies, these teams often rise to the occasion rather than shrink from it.

What fuels a Cinderella run is not magic—it's a potent blend of experience, unity, strategy, and fearless execution that transforms a long shot into a legend.

When Giants Fall: Top Seeds That Crumbled

When top seeds fall in the NCAA Men's Basketball Tournament, the shockwaves are felt across the nation. These teams enter March Madness with high expectations, stellar records, and often national title aspirations. Yet, time and again, they've found themselves on the wrong side of history—defeated by lower-seeded, less heralded opponents in stunning upsets. These collapses are not just surprising; they are defining moments that reshape the tournament, wreck brackets, and become cautionary tales for future contenders. The fall of a giant is dramatic, emotional, and often unforgettable.

One of the most notable collapses occurred in 2018, when No. 1 overall seed Virginia lost to No. 16 seed UMBC. This was the first time in men's tournament history that a 16-seed defeated a 1-seed, and it wasn't a close contest—UMBC won by 20 points. Virginia, known for its methodical offense and elite defense, appeared overwhelmed by UMBC's speed, confidence, and three-point shooting. The upset sent shock and disbelief through the basketball world and showed that even the most disciplined teams could unravel under pressure.

Another painful collapse came in 1991, when 2-seed Syracuse lost to 15-seed Richmond in the First Round. At the time, it was the biggest upset in tournament history. Syracuse, led by legendary coach Jim Boeheim, was expected to cruise past Richmond. However, Richmond's patient offense and tough defense exposed the vulnerabilities of the favored Orange. That game set a precedent and proved that seeding was no guarantee of success.

Kansas, one of college basketball's most storied programs, has experienced several unexpected exits despite entering tournaments as a top seed. In 2010, as a No. 1 seed and heavy favorite, Kansas fell to 9-seed Northern Iowa in the Second Round. The loss was sealed by a deep three-pointer in the final minutes, and the game instantly became one of the most talked-about upsets of the decade. Kansas had one of the most talented rosters in the nation, but Northern Iowa's disciplined play and clutch shooting prevailed.

Gonzaga, often dominant in the regular season, has also faced scrutiny for failing to capitalize on high seeds. In 2013, as a No. 1 seed, Gonzaga lost to 9-seed Wichita State in the Second Round. Despite entering the game with a 32–2 record, Gonzaga struggled to contain Wichita State's perimeter shooting and relentless energy. The loss reinforced the narrative that mid-major dominance doesn't always translate to March success, especially under the weight of national expectations.

These falls are fueled by a range of factors—overconfidence, poor matchups, cold shooting nights, or simply running into a team playing its best basketball at the right moment. The mental toll of carrying the favorite label can lead to tightness, hesitation, and an inability to respond to adversity. Meanwhile, underdogs play with freedom, hunger, and belief.

When giants fall, it's a reminder that March Madness lives up to its name. The unpredictability of the single-elimination format means no team is safe, and no reputation is untouchable. These collapses are part of what makes the tournament so compelling—the notion that every game could be someone's last, no matter how high they've climbed.

Chapter 4
Strategy Behind the Selections

The excitement of March Madness begins long before the first game is played. It starts with the selection process—the moment when 68 teams are chosen and seeded for the NCAA Men's Basketball Tournament. Known as Selection Sunday, this day marks the unveiling of the official bracket and launches a nationwide wave of analysis, debate, and prediction. But behind that one-hour broadcast lies a year's worth of data, scouting, politics, and decision-making. This chapter explores the strategy behind the selections: how teams are evaluated, what criteria matter most, and why some teams are invited while others are left behind.

At the heart of the selection process is the NCAA Selection Committee, a group of athletic directors and conference commissioners representing various institutions across Division I. Their role is to select the 36 at-large teams that did not receive automatic bids, assign all 68 teams a seed from 1 to 16 in each region, and build a balanced, fair bracket. The task is anything but simple. With hundreds of games played across 32 conferences during the season, the committee must evaluate a complex mix of performance indicators, statistical models, and subjective factors to determine which teams have earned a place in the tournament.

The selection process is guided by several core criteria: win-loss records, strength of schedule, quality wins, bad losses, road performance, and performance in conference play. Advanced metrics such as the NCAA Evaluation Tool (NET), KenPom ratings, Sagarin rankings, and the BPI (Basketball Power Index) are all reviewed to assess how well a team has performed relative to its competition. Wins are categorized into "quadrants" based on opponent strength and location, with Quadrant 1 wins—victories against elite teams at home or solid teams on the road—carrying the most weight.

But selection is not just about numbers; it's also about timing and narrative. A team that finishes the season strong or makes a deep run in its conference tournament may boost its chances of being selected or seeded higher. Conversely, a team with a weak non-conference schedule or late-season slump may find itself on the bubble, uncertain whether it will be included. Injuries to key players, coaching changes, and even how a team looks "to the eye" can influence the final decision.

Seeding is another layer of strategy. Teams are grouped into "pods" based on their overall strength, and then placed into the bracket with the goal of creating balanced regions. However, the committee must also avoid early-round rematches, minimize travel where possible, and spread out teams from the same conference. These constraints often force adjustments, meaning a team's seed may not fully reflect its resume, but rather the logistical and structural demands of the bracket.

This chapter will dive into the inner workings of the selection process, the analytical tools used by the committee, the debates that shape final decisions, and the emotional rollercoaster experienced by teams on the bubble. Understanding the strategy behind the selections reveals that March Madness doesn't start with the games—it starts with the bracket, where the fate of every team is decided long before the ball is tipped.

Metrics That Matter: RPI, NET, and Beyond

In the world of NCAA Tournament selections, numbers speak loudly. With dozens of teams vying for limited at-large bids and favorable seedings, metrics play a crucial role in evaluating resumes. Over the years, various statistical models have been developed to help the NCAA Selection Committee assess team performance in a more objective, consistent manner. Among the most important tools are the Ratings Percentage Index (RPI), the NCAA Evaluation Tool (NET), and advanced analytics like KenPom, Sagarin, and the Basketball Power Index (BPI). These systems go beyond simple win-loss records to analyze how, where, and against whom teams have earned their victories.

The RPI was the primary selection metric for decades, emphasizing three factors: a team's winning percentage (25%), its opponents' winning percentage (50%), and its opponents' opponents' winning percentage (25%). The RPI helped gauge strength of schedule and gave weight to beating quality opponents. However, it had limitations. It did not consider scoring margin, game location in depth, or other context-rich data points. As the game evolved and analytics became more advanced, criticism of the RPI grew louder, prompting the NCAA to seek a more comprehensive evaluation model.

Introduced in 2018, the NET replaced the RPI as the NCAA's primary selection tool. The NET incorporates several factors, including game results, strength of schedule, location of games, scoring margin (capped at 10 points to avoid encouraging blowouts), offensive and defensive efficiency, and the quality of wins and losses. Unlike RPI, the NET reflects both a team's results and its performance, offering a more balanced view of how well a team plays—not just who it beats. It is updated daily throughout the season, giving teams a real-time indicator of how they stack up nationally.

A key feature of the NET system is the quadrant system, which divides games into four categories based on opponent strength and game location:

- Quadrant 1: Home vs. Top 30, Neutral vs. Top 50, Away vs. Top 75
- Quadrant 2: Home vs. 31–75, Neutral vs. 51–100, Away vs. 76–135
- Quadrant 3: Home vs. 76–160, Neutral vs. 101–200, Away vs. 136–240
- Quadrant 4: Home vs. 161+, Neutral vs. 201+, Away vs. 241+

Wins in Quadrant 1 are considered the most impressive, while losses in Quadrants 3 and 4 can be damaging. This tiered evaluation allows for a nuanced understanding of a team's resume, considering the context in which games were played.

Beyond NET, committee members often reference KenPom rankings, which evaluate teams based on offensive and defensive efficiency adjusted for pace and strength of opponent. Sagarin ratings factor in win margins, schedule strength, and other statistical indicators, while BPI (developed by ESPN) combines team performance with predictive analytics.

While no single metric guarantees selection or seeding, these tools provide a foundational layer of analysis. They help the committee identify teams that consistently perform at a high level, separate contenders from pretenders, and offer transparency to a process that otherwise relies heavily on subjective debate. In a tournament where every detail matters, metrics serve as the analytical backbone of bracket creation.

Reading the Committee's Mind

Decoding the decisions of the NCAA Selection Committee is both an art and a science. Every year, fans, analysts, and coaches attempt to "read the committee's mind" to understand which teams will make the tournament, how they will be seeded, and what matchups will emerge. While the committee uses official tools and criteria to guide its selections, the process also involves human judgment, debate, and interpretation. Understanding the patterns and priorities that guide the committee's thinking can provide valuable insight into how the bracket takes shape.

At the core of the committee's decision-making process is a team's overall body of work. This includes win-loss record, strength of schedule, key wins, bad losses, road and neutral site performance, and consistency. The committee uses the NCAA Evaluation Tool (NET) as its primary metric, along with supplemental data from KenPom, Sagarin, and other advanced analytics. But raw numbers alone do not dictate decisions. The committee also weighs how a team has performed over time, considering momentum, injuries, and how well the team is playing heading into the tournament.

One key aspect of committee thinking is the value placed on quality wins. A team that defeats multiple high-ranking opponents—especially on the road or in neutral settings—often receives favorable consideration, even if its overall record includes more losses than a comparable team. The quadrant system, particularly Quadrant 1 victories, is essential in evaluating resume strength. A team with several Quadrant 1 wins and few bad losses tends to be rewarded, even if its overall NET ranking is slightly lower than others.

Conversely, bad losses—particularly against Quadrant 3 or 4 opponents—can hurt a team's profile significantly. The committee is quick to penalize teams that lose to weaker competition, especially late in the season when every game carries extra weight. Teams on the bubble often find themselves on the wrong side of the bracket due to one or two damaging losses.

The committee also considers contextual factors, such as injuries to key players or coaching changes. If a team struggled while a star player was injured but performed at a high level when at full strength, the committee may take that into account. However, this is subjective and can vary from year to year, depending on the members' interpretation of fairness and competitiveness.

Another key consideration is conference performance. While no conference is given automatic favoritism, teams from power conferences often benefit from playing more games against top-tier opponents. Mid-major teams with impressive records but fewer quality wins often face more skepticism. The committee must weigh dominance in a weaker conference against competitiveness in a stronger one—a process that can lead to significant debate.

Finally, the committee must consider logistical and structural rules when placing teams. This includes avoiding early-round rematches, keeping teams from the same conference apart until later rounds, and trying to place higher-seeded teams closer to home when possible. These constraints can lead to adjustments in seeding and regional assignments, even for teams with comparable resumes.

Reading the committee's mind involves understanding the balance it tries to strike: honoring statistical performance while applying human judgment. It is a process of alignment, compromise, and justification—where metrics, narratives, and practical realities collide to create the bracket that drives the madness each March.

Public Picks vs. Expert Insights

Every March, as brackets flood offices, group chats, and online contests, two distinct schools of thought emerge: public picks driven by popularity and emotion, and expert insights grounded in data, strategy, and analysis. While both approaches aim to predict the unpredictable NCAA Men's Basketball Tournament, the contrast between them often reveals the tension between perception and performance. Understanding the differences between public sentiment and expert analysis can be the key to building a smarter, more strategic bracket.

Public picks are largely influenced by well-known programs, star players, and recent headlines. Teams like Duke, Kentucky, Kansas, and North Carolina regularly receive a high volume of public support, regardless of their actual seeding or statistical profile in a given year. Familiarity, tradition, and media exposure drive casual fans to select these teams deep into the tournament. Similarly, individual players who have received national attention—whether through highlight reels, viral moments, or award nominations—can sway public opinion even if their overall impact on tournament outcomes is limited.

These selections are also often guided by emotion and narrative. Fans may root for teams with compelling stories, choose based on school allegiance, or pick sentimental favorites. Upsets are frequently predicted based on instinct or superstition rather than matchup analysis. For example, a 12-seed upsetting a 5-seed has become such a common narrative that many fans automatically select one or more 12-over-5 upsets without researching team stats or playing styles.

This herd mentality leads to predictable patterns in public brackets—ones that can be exploited by more informed entries.

Expert insights, on the other hand, are typically based on a deeper evaluation of team performance, advanced metrics, and historical trends. Analysts look at factors such as NET rankings, strength of schedule, offensive and defensive efficiency, bench depth, free throw shooting, and coaching experience. Experts also consider how a team finishes the season, how they perform on neutral courts, and whether their playing style matches up well or poorly with potential opponents.

Experts understand the volatility of certain seed lines and can identify undervalued teams—those whose performance metrics outpace their seeding—as prime upset candidates. They also recognize when highly seeded teams are vulnerable due to weaknesses like over-reliance on one player, lack of defensive consistency, or poor performance away from home. These insights help analysts build more balanced brackets with a blend of smart upsets and safe picks.

The tension between public picks and expert insights becomes most evident in large bracket pools. Public picks tend to cluster around familiar names, meaning choosing differently—when supported by data—can offer a strategic edge. A well-reasoned bracket that avoids popular but shaky favorites and selects overlooked yet efficient teams has a better chance of standing out.

In March Madness, no approach is foolproof. The unpredictable nature of the tournament ensures surprises. But by recognizing the emotional leanings of the public and comparing them with expert-driven analysis, bracket builders can make smarter decisions.

Combining gut feelings with informed research is often the most effective strategy—balancing the madness with method.

Avoiding Common Bracketing Mistakes

Filling out a March Madness bracket is both an exciting tradition and a strategic challenge. With millions of fans participating in pools each year, the difference between a winning bracket and one that collapses in the first weekend often comes down to avoiding common mistakes. Many entries are doomed not because of bad luck, but because of predictable errors made out of habit, emotion, or lack of research. Recognizing and steering clear of these pitfalls can greatly improve the chances of success.

One of the most frequent mistakes is overvaluing name recognition. It's tempting to pick powerhouse programs like Duke, Kentucky, or Kansas to go far every year, simply because they're historically successful. However, past performance does not guarantee future success, especially if a team is having an off-year or is dealing with injuries, inexperience, or inconsistency. Smart bracket builders look at current-season data, not just the name on the jersey.

Another common error is picking too many upsets. While March Madness is known for surprise outcomes, the truth is that most games go according to seeding in the early rounds. People often get caught up in the allure of picking a 13-seed over a 4-seed or predicting a 15-seed Cinderella run. While choosing one or two well-researched upsets can be a smart move, filling a bracket with long-shot picks will more often than not lead to early eliminations. Balance is key—sprinkle in a few upsets, but don't let them dominate your bracket.

The opposite problem also exists: playing it too safe. Some participants avoid picking any upsets at all, sticking strictly to the higher seeds throughout. This strategy usually leads to a decent start but rarely wins large pools. Because some lower-seeded teams almost always win in the First Round, failing to identify any can leave your bracket behind the pack. The goal is to identify upsets that make sense based on matchups, momentum, or style of play—not just pick them randomly or avoid them entirely.

A less obvious mistake is ignoring matchups and playing styles. Basketball is a game of matchups, and some teams are particularly vulnerable to certain styles. For example, a team that relies heavily on a fast-paced offense might struggle against a methodical, defensive-minded opponent. Simply looking at seeding or records without understanding how teams play can lead to bad picks. It's important to research how teams perform against different styles and whether they've been tested against similar opponents.

Another trap is failing to differentiate between bracket strategy and personal fandom. Many fans let their loyalty to a favorite team influence their picks, pushing their alma mater deeper into the tournament than logic would suggest. While it can be fun to root for your team on paper, mixing emotion with prediction often clouds judgment. A good bracket is based on objective reasoning, not wishful thinking.

Finally, not planning for the later rounds can hurt even well-built brackets. Many players focus too much on the First Round and overlook how their Final Four and championship picks will match up. Because most bracket pools award more points in later rounds, having the correct champion and finalists is crucial.

Avoiding these common mistakes won't guarantee victory, but it will provide a strong foundation for making smarter, more competitive bracket choices—turning guesswork into strategy.

Chapter 5
Coaches, Legends, and Game-Changers

Behind every unforgettable March Madness moment lies a figure—or sometimes several—who shapes the outcome far beyond the scoreboard. From tactical masterminds on the sidelines to clutch players who rise to the occasion, the NCAA Men's Basketball Tournament is defined not just by teams, but by individuals who become icons. This chapter explores the coaches, legends, and game-changers whose brilliance, resilience, and impact have transformed the tournament into one of the most celebrated events in sports.

Coaches are the architects of success in March. While talent on the court is essential, it is often the coach's ability to adapt, strategize, and motivate under pressure that makes the difference in a win-or-go-home environment. Some coaches have become synonymous with March Madness itself—names like Mike Krzyzewski, Jim Calhoun, Roy Williams, Tom Izzo, and Rick Pitino evoke memories of championship runs, masterful game plans, and leadership under fire. These men have built dynasties not just with recruiting, but with the kind of experience and poise that can only be earned through years on the tournament stage.

In the heat of March, coaching decisions are magnified. A timely timeout, a late-game substitution, or a surprise defensive adjustment can change the course of a season in seconds. The tournament's single-elimination format allows no margin for error, and coaches must prepare their teams to face unfamiliar opponents, often with only a day or two to prepare. Great coaches rise to this challenge, turning preparation into execution and pressure into performance.

While coaches may set the table, it is often the players who deliver the magic. March Madness has a unique ability to elevate athletes from talented contributors to national legends. Kemba Walker's electrifying 2011 run with UConn, Stephen Curry's breakout performances for Davidson in 2008, and Christian Laettner's iconic buzzer-beater for Duke in 1992 are all reminders that a few extraordinary games can define a career. These players don't just fill up stat sheets—they seize moments, inspire belief, and write history with every shot, steal, and stop.

Beyond the headline names are the unsung heroes—role players who step up when it matters most. A bench player hitting a game-winning three, a lockdown defender shutting down a future NBA star, or a freshman showing veteran poise in a pressure-packed moment—these game-changers remind us that greatness in March can come from anywhere. Their performances often tilt the balance of games and redefine expectations, reinforcing the unpredictable beauty of the tournament.

Game-changers also include those who revolutionize how the game is played. Innovators who popularized the three-point shot, brought the full-court press to national attention, or turned analytics into competitive edges have left lasting marks on the tournament's evolution. Their influence shapes not just individual games, but the entire structure and style of college basketball.

This chapter dives into the stories of these influential figures—the coaches who built empires, the players who captured imaginations, and the change-makers who pushed the game forward.

Together, they are the soul of March Madness, turning strategy into spectacle and possibility into legacy.

Iconic Coaches and Their Legacies

Certain coaches have become inseparable from the legacy of March Madness, not only for the championships they've won but for the indelible impact they've left on the game. These iconic figures are more than just tacticians—they are mentors, motivators, and visionaries who have shaped the identities of their programs and redefined college basketball. Their legacies are built on leadership, innovation, and the ability to consistently elevate their teams when it matters most.

Mike Krzyzewski, better known as "Coach K," is one of the most celebrated figures in NCAA Tournament history. Over his four-decade tenure at Duke University, he led the Blue Devils to five national championships, 13 Final Fours, and a record 1,202 career wins. What set Krzyzewski apart was not just his success but his ability to adapt. Whether he was coaching gritty, experienced rosters in the '90s or embracing one-and-done superstars in the 2010s, Coach K remained competitive through constant evolution. His legacy extends beyond wins—he built a culture of excellence, discipline, and respect that became the blueprint for modern college programs.

John Wooden, the legendary coach of UCLA, is often regarded as the greatest college basketball coach of all time. From 1967 to 1973, his Bruins won seven consecutive national championships—part of a total of 10 titles in 12 years. Wooden's teams were known for their discipline, fundamentals, and execution, but his greatest strength may have been his leadership philosophy. Emphasizing character, preparation, and personal growth, Wooden's "Pyramid of Success" remains a foundational tool for coaches and leaders across all sports.

His calm demeanor and timeless principles continue to influence generations long after his retirement.

Tom Izzo, the longtime coach of Michigan State, has earned a reputation as one of the most reliable March performers in the modern era. With eight Final Four appearances and a national title in 2000, Izzo's teams are known for their physical toughness, rebounding, and defensive grit. What makes Izzo iconic is his consistency—his teams often peak in March regardless of their regular season record. Players improve under his guidance, and his squads are feared for their ability to outwork and outlast opponents when the lights are brightest.

Jim Boeheim of Syracuse built his legacy on longevity and innovation. Coaching the Orange for over 45 years, Boeheim amassed more than 1,000 career wins and led Syracuse to a national championship in 2003. His trademark 2–3 zone defense became one of the most unique and difficult systems for opponents to crack in March. Often underestimated, Boeheim's teams would upset higher seeds, riding their zone defense and timely shot-making deep into the tournament.

Other legends include Dean Smith of North Carolina, who emphasized team play and sportsmanship; Rick Pitino, the first coach to take three different programs to the Final Four; and Jim Calhoun, who built UConn into a national powerhouse from a regional school.

These iconic coaches are more than just winners—they are institutions. Their legacies live on through the players they developed, the programs they built, and the countless coaches they influenced. In the world of March Madness, their names are etched in both history and inspiration.

Players Who Defined the Dance

March Madness has a unique way of turning college basketball players into legends. While many athletes have impressive regular-season careers, it is their performances during the NCAA Tournament that truly define their legacy. The single-elimination format, high-pressure moments, and national spotlight create an environment where players can rise to greatness—or fall short. Those who embrace the challenge and deliver unforgettable performances often etch their names into history. These are the players who defined the Dance—who elevated their teams, captured the hearts of fans, and left lasting impressions on the sport.

Christian Laettner of Duke University is perhaps the most iconic tournament player of all time. He appeared in four straight Final Fours from 1989 to 1992 and won two national championships. His most legendary moment came in the 1992 East Regional Final against Kentucky, where he hit a game-winning buzzer-beater in overtime—a shot that has become one of the most replayed in NCAA history. Laettner's combination of poise, confidence, and clutch performance made him the embodiment of tournament excellence.

Kemba Walker carried the University of Connecticut on his back during the 2011 NCAA Tournament. His magical run began in the Big East Tournament, where he led UConn to five wins in five days, then continued through the national tournament with relentless scoring and leadership. Walker's step-back jumper to beat Pittsburgh in the conference tournament became an instant classic, and he capped it off by leading his team to the national title. His performance is remembered as one of the most dominant and emotionally charged in March Madness history.

Stephen Curry, then an unheralded guard from Davidson College, exploded onto the national scene in 2008. As a sophomore, he led his 10-seed Davidson team to the Elite Eight, defeating powerhouses Gonzaga, Georgetown, and Wisconsin along the way. Curry's deep shooting range, smooth ball-handling, and fearless play turned him into a sensation. Though Davidson fell just short of the Final Four, Curry's run changed how mid-major stars were viewed and paved the way for his future NBA superstardom.

Magic Johnson and Larry Bird redefined college basketball with their showdown in the 1979 national championship game. Johnson's Michigan State team defeated Bird's previously unbeaten Indiana State squad in a game that drew one of the highest television ratings in NCAA history. Their clash not only shaped the future of college basketball but also laid the groundwork for one of the NBA's greatest rivalries.

Carmelo Anthony made a one-year stop at Syracuse University, but his impact was historic. In 2003, as a freshman, Anthony led Syracuse to its first national championship, averaging 20 points and 10 rebounds per game during the tournament. His maturity, versatility, and scoring ability at such a young age marked him as a once-in-a-generation talent.

Other unforgettable performers include Danny Manning (Kansas, 1988), who carried his team to a title and earned the nickname "Danny and the Miracles," and Shane Battier (Duke, 2001), whose leadership and defense anchored a championship run.

These players did more than win games—they created moments that defined eras, inspired future athletes, and contributed to the mystique of March Madness. They didn't just play in the tournament; they became the tournament.

Clutch Performers and Historic Moments

March Madness is synonymous with clutch performances and unforgettable moments. The nature of the NCAA Men's Basketball Tournament—single elimination, national spotlight, and high stakes—creates the perfect conditions for drama. In this crucible, certain players rise above pressure to deliver game-winning shots, heroic efforts, and plays that become etched in college basketball history. These clutch performers and their historic moments embody the very spirit of March Madness: unpredictable, emotional, and electrifying.

One of the most iconic moments in tournament history came in 1992, when Christian Laettner of Duke hit "The Shot" against Kentucky in the East Regional Final. With just 2.1 seconds left in overtime, Grant Hill launched a full-court pass to Laettner, who caught the ball at the free-throw line, faked one way, turned, and nailed a fadeaway jumper as time expired. Laettner finished the game with a perfect 10-for-10 from the field and 10-for-10 from the free-throw line. It was the ultimate clutch performance—delivered on the biggest stage in the most pressure-packed moment.

Another unforgettable moment came in 1983, when Lorenzo Charles of NC State caught a last-second airball and dunked it at the buzzer to defeat Houston's "Phi Slama Jama" team in the national championship game. The dramatic finish gave underdog NC State a 54–52 victory and sparked a wild celebration led by head coach Jim Valvano. It wasn't just the play—it was the story behind it. NC State's Cinderella run and last-second heroics made it one of the most emotional and inspiring endings in tournament history.

Mario Chalmers cemented his legacy with a clutch three-pointer in the 2008 national championship game for Kansas against Memphis.

With his team trailing by three in the final seconds, Chalmers hit a high-arcing shot to send the game into overtime. Kansas went on to win the title, and Chalmers' shot is still remembered as one of the greatest in championship history. It wasn't just the execution—it was the calmness and confidence he showed in a moment that would define his career.

Tate George of UConn added his name to the list of clutch performers with his buzzer-beater against Clemson in the 1990 Sweet 16. With only one second left and his team trailing by one, George caught a full-court pass, turned, and hit a jumper as time expired. The moment became a staple of March Madness highlight reels, showcasing the thin margin between victory and defeat in the tournament.

More recently, Jalen Suggs of Gonzaga delivered one of the most jaw-dropping plays in 2021. In the Final Four against UCLA, Suggs banked in a running 40-foot buzzer-beater in overtime to win the game and send Gonzaga to the championship. The shot was immediately hailed as one of the greatest in tournament history and captured the unfiltered joy and spontaneity that defines March Madness.

These moments are more than just game-winners—they are defining snapshots of the tournament's identity. They remind fans of the emotional highs of victory, the heartbreak of loss, and the pure magic that can happen when preparation meets opportunity. Clutch performers and their historic moments are the pulse of the tournament, making March Madness a truly unforgettable experience year after year.

Coaching Styles That Win in March

In the high-pressure, single-elimination world of March Madness, coaching can be the difference between a first-round exit and a championship run. The NCAA Men's Basketball Tournament rewards not only talent and preparation, but also adaptability, composure, and tactical brilliance. While every coach brings a unique philosophy to the game, certain coaching styles have consistently proven effective during the chaos of March. These approaches share one common goal: putting their teams in the best position to survive and advance.

Defensive-minded coaching has long been a staple of successful tournament teams. Coaches like Tony Bennett at Virginia and Tom Izzo at Michigan State have built programs around defensive toughness and discipline. In March, when nerves are high and offensive efficiency often drops, teams that can rely on solid defense tend to thrive. Bennett's "Pack Line" defense, for example, emphasizes tight help defense and clogging the lane, forcing opponents into tough, contested shots. Izzo's teams, known for their rebounding and physical play, often wear down flashier opponents who aren't prepared for the grind.

Experience-based coaching is another proven method. Coaches who trust veteran players, emphasize mental toughness, and stress execution over flash tend to perform well in tournament play. These coaches often avoid risky or overly complex strategies, instead focusing on fundamentals and staying calm under pressure. Programs that retain players for three or four years often benefit from chemistry, leadership, and maturity—intangibles that make a huge difference in tight games. Coaches like Jay Wright at Villanova used this style to win two national titles in three years (2016 and 2018), relying on experienced, poised rosters that never flinched under pressure.

Adaptability and in-game adjustments are essential traits in coaches who succeed in March. The tournament forces teams to play different styles in quick succession, often with just one day to prepare. Coaches who can adjust their game plans, manage matchups, and exploit opponents' weaknesses in real time have a significant advantage. Bill Self of Kansas is known for his in-game adjustments, whether switching defensive schemes or exploiting mismatches in half-court sets. The ability to stay flexible is crucial when facing unfamiliar teams and unpredictable circumstances.

Guard-oriented coaching is another strategy that pays off in the tournament. Guard play is often the most decisive factor in March—teams with strong backcourts tend to handle pressure better, control tempo, and close games effectively. Coaches who emphasize ball security, perimeter shooting, and leadership from their guards—like former UConn coach Jim Calhoun or current Baylor coach Scott Drew—often see their teams go deep. Having steady guards who can break full-court pressure, make free throws, and execute late-game plays is invaluable.

Motivational leadership also plays a key role. Coaches who can inspire belief and get their players to buy into a common purpose can elevate a team beyond its perceived ceiling. Whether through emotion, culture, or messaging, great coaches find ways to get the best out of their players when it matters most.

Ultimately, there is no one-size-fits-all formula for winning in March, but history shows that toughness, experience, adaptability, and leadership-driven coaching consistently rise to the top. It's not just about drawing up plays—it's about preparing a team to play with heart, intelligence, and resilience when the lights are brightest.

Chapter 6
Fan Frenzy and Office Pools

Every March, something extraordinary happens in offices, classrooms, homes, and sports bars across the country: the arrival of March Madness ignites a nationwide cultural phenomenon. While the NCAA Men's Basketball Tournament is, at its core, a college sports competition, its reach and influence extend far beyond the basketball court. Brackets are printed, predictions are shared, and millions of people—many of whom don't follow college basketball throughout the regular season—suddenly become invested. Chapter 6 explores the unique energy of fan engagement and the massive cultural footprint of office pools, bracket challenges, and the community spirit that makes March Madness more than just a sporting event.

From Selection Sunday to the Final Four, the tournament becomes a shared experience. Whether it's the thrill of watching a buzzer-beater or the heartbreak of a busted bracket, March Madness unites fans and non-fans alike. Part of the magic lies in the bracket itself—a simple, easy-to-understand visual that turns everyone into an analyst. Whether it's a seasoned sports expert using statistical models or a casual fan choosing based on mascots and jersey colors, filling out a bracket becomes an annual ritual. It levels the playing field, creating a fun and often unpredictable competition among friends, coworkers, and strangers.

Office pools are a major driver of the tournament's cultural impact. In many workplaces, productivity dips as employees check scores, stream games during lunch breaks, and root for their picks.

These pools often require little or no entry fee, making them accessible to a broad audience. What starts as a fun team-building activity can quickly evolve into a competitive and highly engaging experience. The office pool is where rivalries form, bragging rights are earned, and even the quietest colleague suddenly becomes a passionate basketball fan.

Online platforms have also elevated bracket culture to new heights. Major sports networks, websites, and apps now host nationwide bracket challenges, offering everything from bragging rights to million-dollar prizes. Social media adds another layer to the madness, as fans share their picks, celebrate wins, lament losses, and react to major upsets in real time. Hashtags trend, memes spread, and viral clips amplify the emotional highs and lows of each game. The tournament becomes a continuous stream of content and conversation, making it one of the most talked-about events of the year.

The fan frenzy goes beyond brackets. Fans proudly wear school colors, organize watch parties, and travel cross-country to support their teams. Student sections become electric with chants and energy, alumni reconnect with pride, and entire cities rally behind Cinderella stories. The passion is infectious, and for many, it's less about the final score and more about being part of something bigger.

This chapter dives into how March Madness became a national celebration, exploring the role of bracket culture, the psychological thrill of competition, and the way the tournament brings people together across generations, backgrounds, and geographies. In the chaos and camaraderie of fan engagement, March Madness transcends basketball—it becomes a collective moment of joy, suspense, and community.

The Rise of Bracketology Culture

Bracketology has evolved from a niche interest into a full-blown cultural phenomenon that captures the imagination of millions every March. What began as a simple exercise in predicting the outcomes of the NCAA Men's Basketball Tournament has grown into a complex, data-driven tradition that blends sports analysis, statistics, competition, and entertainment. The rise of bracketology culture reflects not just a love for college basketball, but a broader human fascination with prediction, patterns, and the thrill of uncertainty.

The term "bracketology" was popularized in the early 2000s by ESPN's Joe Lunardi, who began publishing his tournament predictions online. What started as a fan-driven effort quickly turned into an influential component of the college basketball media ecosystem. Today, bracketologists are viewed as insiders—offering insight into the selection process, seeding logic, and potential matchups before the official bracket is even released on Selection Sunday. Fans follow these experts religiously, debating bubble teams, rooting for "last four in" or "first four out," and obsessing over potential upsets weeks before the tournament begins.

Part of the appeal of bracketology lies in its accessibility. While it incorporates complex data and statistics, it also invites speculation, emotion, and personal bias. Fans can dive deep into NET rankings, strength of schedule, and quadrant wins, or they can go with gut feelings and loyalty to their alma maters. The mix of logic and luck makes it compelling for both analytics-driven enthusiasts and casual participants. Everyone has a shot at a perfect bracket—no matter how improbable—and that dream fuels engagement year after year.

Technology has accelerated the rise of bracketology. Digital platforms now host interactive brackets that automatically update with game results, provide matchup statistics, and allow users to compete in real-time pools with friends or global participants. Websites and apps offer simulations, expert predictions, and user-generated content, turning bracket-filling into an immersive, game-like experience. Even non-sports media outlets now create their own novelty brackets—pitting everything from movie villains to fast food chains against each other—highlighting how the bracket format has transcended sports altogether.

Social media has added another layer of energy to bracketology culture. Twitter becomes a hub of bracket talk, with experts posting "Bracket Watch" updates, fans debating selections, and viral clips from buzzer-beaters fueling arguments over team potential. Platforms like TikTok and Instagram Reels are filled with reaction videos, bracket breakdowns, and comedic takes on tournament drama. This social integration has turned bracketology into not just a private pastime but a shared cultural event.

Bracketology has even influenced how fans consume the tournament itself. Viewers are no longer just rooting for teams—they're rooting for their picks, their pools, their pride. Every game carries personal stakes, making early-round matchups between unfamiliar schools just as exciting as the Final Four. Upsets are celebrated or cursed based on how they affect the bracket, turning every result into an emotional rollercoaster.

In essence, bracketology is more than a prediction game—it's a national ritual. It fuels engagement, deepens fan involvement, and adds layers of meaning to the madness of March. Through analysis, conversation, and competition, it turns basketball into a month-long celebration of sport, chance, and community.

Why Fans Go All-In

Every March, millions of people across the country—and increasingly around the world—go all-in on the NCAA Men's Basketball Tournament. From obsessively researching teams and filling out multiple brackets to rearranging work schedules, attending watch parties, and cheering for unfamiliar schools, fans throw themselves into March Madness with unmatched intensity. But why does this tournament inspire such widespread devotion and emotional investment, even among those who barely follow college basketball the rest of the year?

At the heart of it all is the bracket—a simple, 63-game prediction sheet that turns fans into participants. The bracket gives everyone, regardless of their basketball knowledge, a stake in the outcome. Whether based on advanced metrics or gut instincts, every pick carries weight. With each round, the bracket becomes a personal journey. Every win feels like validation, and every upset feels like heartbreak. It's this emotional rollercoaster that fuels fan passion throughout the tournament.

There's also the appeal of shared experience. March Madness is not just a sports event—it's a cultural one. Office pools, group chats, and friendly rivalries create a sense of camaraderie and competition. People who rarely talk sports suddenly bond over picks, debate seeding controversies, and celebrate—or mourn—their bracket's fate. Watching games together, whether at home, in bars, or on campus, turns the tournament into a social event. The collective excitement builds community and creates lasting memories.

Fans are drawn to the tournament's unpredictability. Unlike professional playoffs that span weeks or months with best-of-seven series, March Madness is a single-elimination format—every game is win or go home. This intensity raises the stakes and makes every minute matter. Cinderella stories, buzzer-beaters, and shocking upsets are not only possible—they're expected. Fans go all-in because they know that in March, anything can happen, and often does.

There's also something inherently appealing about the underdog narrative. Fans love seeing small schools topple giants, unknown players become overnight heroes, and unheralded teams go on improbable runs. These storylines tap into universal human emotions: hope, resilience, and the desire to overcome odds. Rooting for the underdog, even if it means risking your bracket's success, is part of what makes the tournament so emotionally compelling.

For many fans, school pride and tradition play a big role. Alumni and students rally behind their teams with unmatched loyalty, donning school colors, chanting fight songs, and following every game with religious devotion. The tournament becomes a reflection of identity—personal, regional, and institutional. Even fans without a direct connection to a school are drawn to its traditions, mascots, and style of play.

Finally, media coverage and technology have amplified the experience. Games are streamed on multiple platforms, scores are updated in real time, and social media allows instant reactions. Highlights, commentary, memes, and debates circulate constantly, making it easy for fans to stay engaged.

In the end, fans go all-in because March Madness offers something rare in sports: pure, unscripted drama where everyone has a role to play. It's more than basketball—it's a shared celebration of unpredictability, passion, and connection.

Inside the Billion-Dollar Bracket Challenge

The idea of winning a billion dollars for filling out a perfect NCAA Tournament bracket sounds like fantasy—but in 2014, it briefly became reality. When Warren Buffett, in collaboration with Quicken Loans, announced the Billion-Dollar Bracket Challenge, it captured national attention and forever changed how fans viewed bracket competitions. Though no one came close to claiming the prize, the challenge tapped into the already-thriving bracket culture and highlighted just how big the business behind March Madness had become.

At its core, the Billion-Dollar Bracket Challenge promised $1 billion to anyone who could correctly predict the outcome of all 63 games of the NCAA Men's Basketball Tournament. On the surface, it sounded like a once-in-a-lifetime opportunity. In reality, the odds of filling out a perfect bracket are astronomical—estimated at 1 in 9.2 quintillion if picks are made randomly, or about 1 in 120 billion with some basketball knowledge. Those numbers didn't deter millions of hopefuls from entering the contest, each believing that, somehow, their bracket might defy the odds.

The challenge quickly became a viral sensation. News outlets across the country ran stories, social media exploded with bracket-building strategies, and office pools took on a new level of competitiveness. People who had never watched a full college basketball game suddenly became invested analysts. Bracketology, already a growing phenomenon, was elevated into the mainstream in a way never seen before.

But beyond the hype, the challenge was a savvy marketing move. Quicken Loans used the competition to collect data from entrants, offering up to 15 million dollars in consolation prizes, including

$100,000 each to the top 20 closest brackets. Participants were required to provide personal information, which allowed Quicken to generate leads for its mortgage business. Warren Buffett, through his firm Berkshire Hathaway, insured the billion-dollar prize—an example of how risk and reward in finance can be cleverly tied to cultural events.

The challenge also shone a light on the economic scale of March Madness. The tournament generates over a billion dollars annually through television rights, advertising, sponsorships, and ticket sales. Companies like CBS and Turner Sports pay huge sums to broadcast the games, and advertisers scramble for airtime during the most-watched matchups. Bracket competitions like the Billion-Dollar Challenge became extensions of this economic engine, drawing in even more viewers and engagement.

While no one has since attempted to offer a billion-dollar prize on that scale again, its legacy remains. Bracket contests are now an integral part of digital engagement strategies for companies across industries. Sportsbooks, tech platforms, and even fast-food chains run bracket challenges to build brand awareness and drive traffic. Buffett himself still offers a more modest bracket incentive to employees of his companies—typically $1 million per year for a perfect Sweet 16.

The Billion-Dollar Bracket Challenge proved that the madness of March isn't limited to the court. It's about imagination, strategy, and the chance—however small—of achieving the impossible. It reminded everyone that for three wild weeks each spring, even the most impossible dream can feel just one pick away.

The Social and Psychological Side of Competing

While March Madness is rooted in college basketball, its influence reaches far beyond sports. For millions of participants, the

NCAA Tournament becomes a psychological and social experience that engages emotions, relationships, and identity. Whether filling out brackets for office pools, joining fantasy-style contests with friends, or simply following their favorite teams, fans invest more than just time—they invest themselves. The social and psychological side of competing in March Madness reveals why the tournament has such powerful appeal, and why so many return to the bracket year after year.

One of the most compelling psychological elements is the illusion of control. Even though the tournament is unpredictable, with upsets and surprises nearly guaranteed, fans still feel empowered when making their bracket choices. The process of researching teams, analyzing statistics, and selecting winners gives participants a sense of agency. Picking a low seed to upset a favorite and watching it happen feels like validation—not just of basketball knowledge, but of decision-making ability. This perceived control is satisfying, even when the outcome is partially or largely based on chance.

Closely related is the psychological principle of risk and reward. Filling out a bracket is essentially a game of prediction, and the thrill of getting a pick right—especially a risky upset—triggers the brain's reward system. Dopamine levels rise with each correct guess, and this pleasure reinforces continued engagement. For many, it's not about winning a prize; it's about the internal satisfaction of outsmarting the field or beating friends and coworkers. The emotional highs and lows mimic those found in gambling or video games, making the tournament intensely engaging.

Socially, March Madness fosters connection and camaraderie. Bracket competitions and office pools create friendly rivalries and group bonding. Coworkers who rarely interact suddenly find themselves talking strategy or teasing each other about picks. Families create traditions around the tournament, watching games together and tracking their brackets on the fridge. These shared experiences strengthen relationships and foster a sense of belonging. Even among strangers, the tournament acts as a conversation starter, turning casual fans into part of a larger community.

At the same time, March Madness taps into our desire for narrative and identity. Fans often root for teams that reflect aspects of themselves—their alma mater, hometown heroes, or underdog stories that align with personal values. Watching a small, overlooked school take down a national powerhouse feels emotionally satisfying not just because it's surprising, but because it symbolizes hope, grit, and justice. People project their own stories onto the tournament, making it deeply personal.

March Madness also plays into competitive instincts. Whether it's winning the office pool, beating a sibling, or proving your bracket is better than a pundit's, the tournament satisfies a basic human drive: the desire to win. But it does so in a lighthearted, low-risk way. The stakes are mostly emotional, which makes the competition fun rather than stressful.

Ultimately, the social and psychological dimensions of March Madness explain why it captures so much attention. It's more than basketball—it's a communal, emotional journey that allows people to connect, compete, and feel a part of something bigger than themselves.

Chapter 7
The Evolution of the Game

The NCAA Men's Basketball Tournament has long been celebrated for its tradition, pageantry, and raw excitement. But beneath the surface of buzzer-beaters and Cinderella stories lies a deeper, ongoing transformation—the evolution of the game itself. Over the decades, college basketball has shifted dramatically in terms of play style, player development, technology, and even tournament structure. What began in 1939 as an eight-team competition has grown into a 68-team national phenomenon, reflecting the broader changes in sports, media, and culture.

This chapter explores the multifaceted evolution of the game, from the way basketball is played to the way it's experienced by fans, athletes, and institutions. The pace, strategy, and skillsets that define modern college basketball are markedly different from those of earlier eras. Shot clocks, three-point lines, and positionless basketball have all reshaped how the sport is approached tactically. Coaches and players must now adapt to a faster, more dynamic version of the game, where versatility and perimeter shooting often outweigh size and brute strength.

Beyond the hardwood, the player experience has also undergone significant change. Today's college athletes are more visible, more empowered, and more prepared than ever before. Elite high school prospects often arrive on campus as fully developed brands, thanks in part to social media, grassroots basketball circuits, and increased national exposure. The introduction of Name, Image, and Likeness

(NIL) legislation has further transformed the landscape, allowing student-athletes to monetize their fame and opening new avenues for endorsement, marketing, and influence—all while still competing at the collegiate level.

Technology has also played a transformative role in the evolution of college basketball. Analytics are now central to decision-making, from recruiting to in-game adjustments. Coaching staffs rely on advanced statistics to break down opponent tendencies, evaluate performance, and maximize efficiency. Video analysis tools have become standard, giving teams the ability to fine-tune every possession. The influence of data has pushed the game toward more calculated, strategic approaches, changing how coaches build game plans and how players train and perform.

Meanwhile, the tournament itself has evolved in structure and presentation. The expansion from 64 to 68 teams introduced the First Four, adding another layer of opportunity and excitement. Broadcast coverage has grown exponentially, with every game now available to watch live across multiple platforms. Social media and digital engagement have made March Madness a real-time, immersive experience that extends far beyond television. The tournament has become a global event, followed not just for the basketball, but for its cultural and commercial impact.

This chapter examines these sweeping changes in detail, tracing how the game has grown, adapted, and modernized without losing the core spirit that makes March Madness special. From rule changes and recruiting shifts to media innovations and athlete empowerment, we'll explore how the evolution of the game continues to shape the tournament—and why that evolution is key to keeping March Madness relevant, thrilling, and truly mad in every era.

How College Basketball Has Changed

College basketball has undergone a profound transformation over the past several decades, evolving in ways that have reshaped how the game is played, coached, experienced, and consumed. From the introduction of the shot clock and three-point line to changes in recruiting, player development, and media exposure, the sport has adapted to cultural, technological, and institutional shifts. These changes have not only impacted the quality and pace of play but also the way fans engage with the NCAA Tournament and college basketball as a whole.

One of the most visible changes has been in playing style. Early college basketball emphasized slow, methodical ball movement and interior play, often resulting in low-scoring affairs. The game was dominated by big men, with post-ups and mid-range jumpers defining offensive strategy. That changed with the introduction of the shot clock in 1985, which forced teams to play at a quicker pace and created more possessions. The adoption of the three-point line in 1986 further revolutionized offensive philosophy, making spacing, perimeter shooting, and guard play more central to team success. Today's game is faster, more fluid, and more reliant on the three-pointer than ever before.

Another major shift has come in player development and mobility. In previous eras, players typically stayed in college for three or four years, allowing teams to develop cohesion and giving fans the chance to build long-term connections with athletes. Now, with the rise of the one-and-done era—where top players leave for the NBA after just one season—rosters turn over more quickly, and programs must constantly reload. In addition, the transfer portal has made it easier than ever for players to switch schools, giving athletes more freedom but also challenging coaches to maintain continuity and chemistry.

Athlete empowerment has reached new levels with the introduction of Name, Image, and Likeness (NIL) legislation. Student-athletes can now earn money through endorsements, sponsorships, and social media, reshaping the college basketball landscape. This shift has altered recruiting dynamics and changed the perception of amateurism in college sports. Players are no longer just athletes—they are public figures and personal brands, managing both on-court performance and off-court opportunities.

The rise of analytics and technology has also changed how the game is approached. Coaches and analysts now use data to evaluate shot quality, defensive efficiency, and player tendencies in far greater detail than ever before. Practices are recorded, broken down frame by frame, and optimized through performance tracking systems. Game planning has become more strategic, with decisions increasingly guided by data rather than gut instinct.

Meanwhile, media coverage and fan engagement have exploded. Where games were once only available on regional TV, now every tournament game is streamed nationally, with fans able to watch from anywhere on any device. Social media platforms have turned players into online personalities and made the tournament a constant, interactive conversation. Bracket culture, viral highlights, and real-time reactions have all added new dimensions to how college basketball is consumed and celebrated.

In sum, college basketball has shifted from a regional, tradition-bound sport into a fast-paced, media-driven, player-centric spectacle. These changes continue to redefine what it means to play, coach, and watch the game—and they keep the madness of March as relevant and exciting as ever.

The One-and-Done Era

The "one-and-done" era has been one of the most transformative and debated phases in the history of college basketball. This term refers to the trend of elite high school players attending college for a single season before declaring for the NBA Draft. Sparked by a 2006 NBA rule change that required players to be at least one year removed from high school before entering the draft, the one-and-done model quickly became a pipeline for top-tier talent—and a flashpoint in the evolving relationship between amateurism and professional aspirations.

Prior to the rule change, players could jump straight from high school to the NBA, as seen with legends like Kobe Bryant, Kevin Garnett, and LeBron James. But in an effort to better prepare athletes physically and mentally, the NBA and its players' association instituted the age restriction. The result was a flood of top recruits enrolling in college programs for one mandatory year—long enough to showcase their talent, boost their draft stock, and move on to the pros.

This shift dramatically altered the recruiting landscape. Programs with national visibility and strong NBA connections, such as Kentucky, Duke, and Kansas, began to dominate the recruitment of one-and-done athletes. Coaches tailored their strategies to accommodate short-term talent, building rosters with high ceilings but limited continuity. John Calipari at Kentucky, in particular, embraced the model, guiding a revolving door of elite freshmen to deep tournament runs and NBA success. His 2012 national championship team, led by freshman Anthony Davis, became the prototype of what a one-and-done roster could achieve.

However, the era has been met with criticism and concern. Detractors argue that the system undermines the academic mission of college sports, with athletes often attending school for just a semester before focusing solely on the draft. Some believe it contributes to a lack of team chemistry, as constant roster turnover can hinder development and long-term cohesion. Fans have also expressed frustration at not being able to watch their favorite players grow over several seasons.

Despite these concerns, the one-and-done era has undeniably raised the level of talent in college basketball. Even short stints from players like Kevin Durant (Texas), Zion Williamson (Duke), and Derrick Rose (Memphis) brought excitement, television ratings, and increased visibility to the sport. These stars captivated audiences and provided unforgettable tournament moments, even if their time in college was brief.

The era has also influenced the NCAA's structure and policies. With increasing calls for reform and the rise of alternatives like the NBA G League Ignite program, overseas contracts, and NIL opportunities, the future of one-and-done is uncertain. The NBA has discussed lowering the age limit again, which could re-open the door for high school players to go pro directly—effectively ending the one-and-done pipeline.

In the meantime, the one-and-done era remains a defining chapter in the story of modern college basketball. It has reshaped recruiting, altered program-building philosophies, and blurred the lines between amateur and professional sports. Love it or criticize it, this era has left an undeniable mark on the madness of March.

Three-Point Revolution and Positionless Play

The landscape of college basketball has dramatically shifted in recent years, with two of the most impactful changes being the rise of the three-point revolution and the embrace of positionless play. These developments have not only transformed how teams approach offense and defense but have also redefined player roles, recruiting priorities, and game strategy—particularly in the high-stakes environment of March Madness.

The three-point line, introduced to NCAA basketball in 1986, was initially seen as a novelty—a tool for spacing the floor and giving underdogs a chance to catch up quickly. But over the decades, and especially in the last 15 years, it has become a cornerstone of offensive strategy. Inspired in part by trends in the NBA, where teams now prioritize spacing and outside shooting, college coaches began adapting their systems to include more perimeter-based play. Today, it's not uncommon for teams to attempt 25 to 30 three-pointers in a single game. Programs like Villanova, Gonzaga, and Baylor have all used the three-point shot as a weapon to spread defenses thin, open up driving lanes, and generate efficient scoring opportunities.

This three-point revolution has leveled the playing field in many ways. Teams without dominant big men can now rely on perimeter shooting and ball movement to compete against more physically imposing opponents. In tournament play, where upsets are frequent, the three-point shot gives lower-seeded teams a legitimate path to victory. A hot shooting night from beyond the arc can completely neutralize a size or talent disparity—one of the reasons March Madness remains so unpredictable and thrilling.

Parallel to this trend is the rise of positionless basketball—a style of play where traditional positions like point guard, shooting guard, and power forward are less rigid. In today's game, players are expected to be versatile: guards need to rebound and defend multiple positions, while forwards are often capable of handling the ball, passing, and shooting from distance. This shift has created more fluid offenses and switch-heavy defensive schemes, allowing teams to adapt quickly and exploit mismatches.

Positionless play has changed recruiting philosophies as well. Coaches now look for players with length, mobility, and a diverse skill set rather than pigeonholing athletes into conventional roles. A 6'8" forward who can shoot threes, defend guards, and initiate offense is now more valuable than a traditional post player limited to paint scoring. This evolution is particularly evident in programs like Michigan, Iowa State, and Houston, which have built successful teams around interchangeable lineups and dynamic, multi-skilled athletes.

The combination of three-point shooting and positionless play has also increased the pace of games. Transition offenses, spread pick-and-rolls, and five-out sets are now common. Defensively, teams are switching more frequently and relying on versatile defenders who can guard multiple positions, reflecting a shift toward adaptability and speed.

Together, these trends have made college basketball more exciting, faster, and tactically complex. They've empowered underdogs, expanded what's possible on the court, and made March Madness even more chaotic and captivating. As the game continues to evolve, one thing is clear: the era of traditional roles and paint-dominated play is giving way to a new, more dynamic version of basketball.

Impact of NIL and Transfer Portal

The landscape of college basketball has been reshaped in profound ways by two transformative developments: Name, Image, and Likeness (NIL) rights and the expansion of the transfer portal. Together, they have ushered in a new era of athlete empowerment, recruitment dynamics, and program-building strategies. These changes have impacted not only how teams are assembled but also how players make decisions, how fans engage with athletes, and how the NCAA Tournament itself is experienced.

Name, Image, and Likeness (NIL) legislation, implemented in 2021, allows college athletes to profit from endorsements, sponsorships, merchandise sales, appearances, and social media partnerships. For decades, players contributed to a billion-dollar industry without any direct compensation. Now, athletes can monetize their personal brands while still competing at the collegiate level. This change has been a game-changer, particularly for basketball players, who often have high visibility, large social media followings, and marketability both locally and nationally.

NIL has shifted the recruiting landscape dramatically. While elite athletes were always drawn to major programs, NIL opportunities have added a new layer of consideration. Some players now weigh not only a school's basketball pedigree but also its media market, alumni network, and NIL infrastructure. Programs that can offer strong brand-building support, business education, and access to sponsors have a significant edge. As a result, schools in big cities or with major national platforms have increased appeal—even to prospects who might not have previously considered them.

Mid-major players have also benefited. Standout performers at smaller programs can now attract attention from businesses in their communities, allowing them to build financial security while staying closer to home or delaying professional aspirations. In some cases, NIL deals have encouraged players to stay in college longer, helping maintain program stability and elevating the overall talent level across the sport.

Simultaneously, the transfer portal has revolutionized player movement. Previously, transferring required athletes to sit out a year unless they received a waiver. Now, with the one-time transfer rule, players can move freely without losing eligibility. This has made the portal a central hub of the offseason, with hundreds of athletes exploring new opportunities each year.

The transfer portal has created a more fluid, fast-paced environment for roster management. Coaches must now recruit not only high school players but also existing college athletes—and retain their own rosters amid growing competition. For players, the portal provides a way to find better fits, earn more playing time, or join programs with better exposure or NIL potential. Some teams have even rebuilt entire rosters in a single offseason using the portal, leading to more parity and unpredictability in tournament play.

However, both NIL and the transfer portal have sparked debate. Critics argue that the system resembles free agency and undermines the idea of amateurism and team loyalty. Supporters counter that players finally have agency and compensation in a system that has long profited from their efforts.

Ultimately, the impact of NIL and the transfer portal has been transformative. They've redefined power dynamics in college basketball, shifted how programs compete, and added new storylines to March Madness. The result is a sport more dynamic, unpredictable, and player-driven than ever before.

Chapter 8
Building the Perfect Bracket

Every March, as Selection Sunday unveils the NCAA Men's Basketball Tournament bracket, millions of fans, analysts, and casual participants alike embark on the same thrilling, daunting challenge: building the perfect bracket. It's a pursuit that blends logic and instinct, data and emotion, strategy and superstition. While the dream of a truly flawless bracket remains elusive—with odds of perfection estimated at 1 in 9.2 quintillion—the process of trying has become a beloved national tradition. This chapter dives into the art and science of building the perfect bracket, examining what it takes to make smart picks, avoid common traps, and outwit both your competition and the chaos of March Madness.

The bracket itself is a puzzle—63 games, each one a potential landmine or opportunity. The beauty of the bracket lies in its simplicity: two teams, one advances. But beneath that simplicity is a web of complexity. A smart pick in one game may affect later rounds; a single early-round upset can unravel your Final Four. Building the perfect bracket means thinking ahead, balancing risk and reward, and choosing where to be bold and where to play it safe.

Fans approach bracket-building in various ways. Some follow their hearts, picking based on alma maters, mascots, or jersey colors. Others rely on analytics—evaluating seeding, team metrics, offensive and defensive efficiency, and performance in "Quadrant 1" games. Then there are the bracketologists and data wizards who crunch numbers, run simulations, and apply predictive models to every matchup. Despite the range of approaches, no method has proven foolproof, and every tournament delivers unexpected results that shake even the most meticulously crafted brackets.

Key to building a strong bracket is understanding tournament dynamics. Upsets are a hallmark of March Madness, but predicting which lower-seeded teams will break through requires careful study. Which 12-seed has a strong backcourt? Which 4-seed relies too heavily on one player? Which team underperformed during the regular season but is peaking at the right time? These kinds of insights help bracket-builders identify smart risks—those underdogs that have a legitimate path to the second weekend.

Another critical element is regional analysis. Not all regions are created equal; some are top-heavy with elite programs, while others are wide open. Identifying which regions are more likely to produce chaos—and which are more likely to hold form—can give you an edge. The same goes for analyzing coaching experience, guard play, free-throw shooting, and how well teams perform away from home—all factors that can tip close games.

In this chapter, we'll explore proven strategies for crafting a winning bracket, from studying matchups and identifying upset potential to making smart Final Four and championship picks. We'll also examine psychological traps that often lead to bracket busts, such as overvaluing favorites, ignoring late-season momentum, or making emotional decisions. While perfection may be impossible, building a smart, resilient, and competitive bracket is well within reach—and doing so makes every game more meaningful and every win more satisfying.

Because in March, the only thing more thrilling than watching the madness unfold is knowing you saw it coming.

Data-Driven Decision Making

In the age of analytics, data-driven decision making has become one of the most powerful tools for building a successful NCAA Tournament bracket. While gut instinct and emotional loyalty still drive many casual picks, those who consistently perform well in bracket competitions increasingly rely on statistics, historical patterns, and advanced metrics to guide their choices. In a tournament where surprises are expected and one game can change everything, using data as a compass can help bracket-builders navigate the chaos with clarity.

The first step in data-driven bracketology is understanding the predictive metrics used to evaluate team performance. Tools like the NCAA Evaluation Tool (NET), KenPom rankings, Sagarin ratings, and Barttorvik efficiency ratings give deep insight into a team's strengths and weaknesses. These systems measure offensive and defensive efficiency, pace of play, strength of schedule, and performance in various game environments (home, road, neutral). Rather than relying solely on seeding or win-loss records, these analytics provide a fuller picture of how well a team is actually performing.

One of the most useful applications of this data is identifying vulnerable high seeds. A team with a high seed but poor defensive metrics or a weak record in Quadrant 1 games (games against strong opponents) may be ripe for an upset. Conversely, a lower-seeded team with a top-20 efficiency rating or a strong showing in close games might be a hidden gem. Analytics help strip away bias and reputation, allowing bracket builders to see teams for what they are — statistical profiles, not just big names.

Another data-driven approach is trend analysis. For example, since the tournament expanded to 64 teams in 1985, at least one 12-seed has beaten a 5-seed in nearly 70% of tournaments. Knowing this doesn't mean picking every 12-seed to win, but it signals that you should look closely at those matchups. Other trends show that teams with top-25 adjusted defensive efficiency often make deep runs, while teams overly reliant on three-point shooting can be vulnerable to off-nights.

Injury reports and late-season momentum also factor into a data-smart strategy. A team that starts the season strong but fades in February may be less reliable than a squad peaking at the right time. Similarly, the loss or return of a key player can drastically affect a team's tournament outlook—something that may not be reflected in their overall record but will show up in recent game metrics.

Data also helps in forecasting the later rounds. Rather than focusing only on the First Round, bracket success usually hinges on picking the correct Final Four and champion. Teams that rank in the top 20 in both offensive and defensive efficiency—often referred to as "two-way teams"—are statistically more likely to win the title. Identifying these balanced squads early can help build a resilient bracket.

In a tournament where chaos is inevitable, data provides structure. While it won't predict every upset or buzzer-beater, it offers the best possible foundation for smart, informed decisions. By blending historical trends, current performance metrics, and matchup analysis, data-driven decision making turns March Madness from a guessing game into a strategic challenge.

Balancing Risk and Reward

One of the most essential elements of successful bracket-building during March Madness is balancing risk and reward. Every game is an opportunity to gain points—or lose them—and with millions of brackets competing in pools nationwide, choosing when to take a chance and when to play it safe becomes a strategic art. A bracket that's too conservative may survive early rounds but rarely wins large pools. On the other hand, one filled with wild upsets may flame out quickly. Striking the right balance can separate a busted bracket from a winning one.

At the core of this balance is understanding where and when to take risks. First-round upsets are a staple of March Madness. Every year, lower-seeded teams surprise favorites, and correctly picking one or two of these games can give your bracket a major edge. However, data shows that most upsets happen within specific seed ranges—such as 12-seeds beating 5-seeds or 11-seeds defeating 6-seeds. Instead of randomly choosing longshots, bracket-builders should target specific matchups where an upset is both statistically and stylistically likely. A well-researched upset pick is a calculated risk, not a gamble.

The key is strategic differentiation. In a small pool, a safe and conservative bracket with a few intelligent upset picks may be enough to win. But in larger, more competitive pools, it often takes bold moves to stand out. This might mean picking a non-top seed to make a Final Four run or selecting an unconventional national champion. If that team performs well, you've gained a significant edge over others who stuck with popular choices. But this only pays off if those risks are informed, not impulsive.

It's also important to play it safe where it matters most. Later-round games—Sweet 16, Elite Eight, Final Four, and the Championship—are worth the most points in most bracket formats. This is where most upsets stop and higher seeds typically prevail. Choosing too many Cinderella teams to go deep can destroy a bracket's long-term value. Historical data supports that national champions usually come from top three seeds and are often balanced teams with both strong offense and defense.

Hedging your bracket is another way to manage risk. For instance, if you choose a major upset in one region, you might want to go more conservative in another. This diversification means that one wrong pick won't sink your entire bracket. It also allows for recovery—if one risk doesn't pay off, a solid performance from your more predictable picks can keep you in the running.

Emotion is a risk in itself. Many bracket-makers pick with their hearts—choosing their alma mater, a favorite coach, or a sentimental underdog. While passion can make the experience more fun, overcommitting to emotional picks is a common path to a busted bracket. Discipline, even in the face of personal bias, is what separates casual picks from smart strategies.

Ultimately, balancing risk and reward in March Madness is about making bold, thoughtful decisions while protecting the core strength of your bracket. It's about taking chances where it counts—and avoiding recklessness where it doesn't. Success comes not from playing it safe or going all-in, but from knowing when to do both.

Dark Horse Picks and Final Four Predictions

In the unpredictable world of March Madness, the allure of dark horse picks and bold Final Four predictions is undeniable. Every tournament features a team—or several—that defy expectations, bust brackets, and capture national attention. While top seeds dominate the championship conversation, it's often the under-the-radar teams, the ones just outside the spotlight, that make the biggest impact. Identifying these dark horses and making smart Final Four predictions can be the difference between an average bracket and a championship-winning one.

A dark horse isn't necessarily a Cinderella team seeded 12 or lower. Often, it's a 4 to 8 seed that has the tools to make a deep run but isn't being widely discussed. These teams tend to fly under the radar due to late-season losses, tough conference competition, or lack of national media attention. However, what they often have are the essential ingredients for tournament success: experienced guards, a strong coach, defensive tenacity, and momentum.

History offers several examples. Loyola Chicago (2018) made the Final Four as an 11-seed with a veteran-laden roster and a smart, methodical style of play. South Carolina (2017), a 7-seed, shocked the field with suffocating defense and fearless energy. More recently, Miami and San Diego State (2023) proved that teams outside the top seed lines could outwork and outmatch blueblood programs when it counts most. Spotting such teams before the bracket locks in can give your picks a unique edge.

When considering dark horses, look for a few key factors:

1. Strong guard play – Guards control tempo, manage pressure, and often decide close games.
2. Elite defense – Teams that can force turnovers, rebound well, and defend without fouling tend to survive tough matchups.
3. Balance and depth – One-dimensional teams or those relying on a single star often struggle in March.

4. Quality wins – A resume with solid wins over tournament-caliber opponents signals readiness for the big stage.
5. Experienced coaching – A coach who can adjust mid-game and prepare for varied opponents is invaluable in a single-elimination format.

When it comes to Final Four predictions, balance is key. While it's tempting to go chalk and pick all No. 1 seeds, this rarely plays out. In most years, at least one lower seed reaches the Final Four. The challenge is identifying which one.

A smart Final Four typically includes:

- One or two top seeds: Programs that have shown consistency, have NBA-level talent, and rank high in both offensive and defensive efficiency.
- One mid-tier seed (3–6): A team with underappreciated metrics or a favorable path through their region.
- One wild card: A bold pick that matches the profile of a dark horse—a team with potential to surprise.

Also consider matchups within the region. Some teams have paths that bypass stylistic nightmares or draw opponents that play into their strengths. A good bracket isn't about being perfect; it's about being ahead of the curve.

In the end, mixing solid logic with a bit of boldness leads to a Final Four that is both competitive and unique. Embrace the uncertainty, but do your homework—because one right dark horse pick can be what sets your bracket apart from the rest.

Tools and Apps for Modern Bracketeers

In the digital age, bracket-building has evolved from a pen-and-paper ritual into a high-tech, data-driven experience. Today's "bracketeers" have access to a wide array of tools, apps, and platforms that provide in-depth analytics, real-time updates, expert analysis, and interactive features designed to help users craft smarter, more competitive NCAA Tournament brackets. Whether you're a casual fan trying to win the office pool or a seasoned veteran aiming for national contests, using the right digital tools can give you a significant edge.

One of the most widely used platforms is ESPN's Tournament Challenge. With millions of entries each year, it's the gold standard for online bracket pools. The platform is user-friendly, allows for multiple entries, and offers features like automatic scoring updates, expert picks, and percentage breakdowns that show how the public is voting on each matchup. These percentages are especially useful for bracketeers trying to zig when others zag, creating differentiation in larger pools.

CBS Sports also offers a highly polished bracket experience. Their app includes access to video highlights, matchup analysis, expert commentary, and a "Bracket Manager" tool that simplifies pool creation and scoring for groups. The CBS app is particularly helpful for following live games while tracking the performance of your bracket in real time.

Yahoo Sports provides another strong platform for bracket play, especially for those who want a more casual and social experience. Yahoo's bracket tool integrates well with email invites and social media, making it easy to challenge friends and family. Its clean interface and real-time stats make it a popular choice for group play.

For users who want to go beyond mainstream platforms and dive deep into analytics and predictions, sites like KenPom.com and Barttorvik.com are invaluable. These websites offer detailed efficiency metrics, adjusted offensive and defensive ratings, and player-level data. Advanced users can simulate potential matchups, evaluate upset potential, and compare teams across a range of variables. While KenPom requires a small subscription fee, its predictive power is widely respected among serious bracketeers.

TeamRankings.com is another favorite among data-driven players. It provides bracket picks based on statistical models, customizable bracket generators, and pool-specific strategy tools. One standout feature is the ability to tailor your bracket picks based on your pool's size and scoring rules, helping you maximize your chances in different formats.

Mobile apps like Bracket HQ and PocketBracket are perfect for users looking to build brackets on the go. These apps offer intuitive drag-and-drop functionality, live scoring updates, and customizable tournament simulations. Many also include historical tournament data to inform your decisions based on past trends.

Finally, social media platforms like Twitter, Reddit (especially r/CollegeBasketball), and YouTube offer real-time insights, debates, and predictions from fans, analysts, and insiders. Following beat reporters, bracketologists, and data scientists can expose you to valuable last-minute information—like injury reports or unexpected line-up changes—that might influence your picks.

In today's tournament landscape, building a great bracket is no longer about guesswork alone. With the right tools and apps, modern bracketeers can combine instinct with insight—transforming March Madness into a well-informed, high-stakes strategic game.

Chapter 9
Broadcasting the Madness

Every spring, the NCAA Men's Basketball Tournament becomes one of the most-watched sporting events in the world. But beyond the thrilling buzzer-beaters, Cinderella runs, and championship celebrations lies a powerful engine that brings March Madness into homes, offices, and mobile screens across the globe: the broadcast. From radio announcers and television crews to digital streamers and social media live feeds, the way March Madness is consumed has changed dramatically over the decades. Chapter 9 explores how the tournament has evolved into a multimedia spectacle, how broadcasting shaped the event's popularity, and why it continues to be one of the most valuable properties in sports media.

When the NCAA Tournament began in 1939, it was a modest eight-team affair with limited media attention. Fast forward to today, and it has become a billion-dollar media enterprise, with every game aired live, often on multiple platforms simultaneously. The transformation began with the expansion of television coverage in the 1980s, particularly through CBS Sports, which recognized the tournament's dramatic potential and invested in turning it into a national event. In 2010, the NCAA struck a groundbreaking deal with CBS and Turner Sports, bringing TNT, TBS, and truTV into the broadcasting fold and ensuring that every game of the tournament would be televised live—an unprecedented move in American sports.

This coverage revolutionized the fan experience. No longer limited to just regional broadcasts or highlight packages, fans could now follow every game, every upset, and every storyline in real time. With wall-to-wall coverage, the opening Thursday and Friday of the tournament became unofficial national holidays, with millions tuning in from workplaces, classrooms, and living rooms to catch the action. The ability to follow multiple games at once changed how viewers interacted with the tournament, turning it into an immersive, multi-screen experience.

In recent years, digital streaming has taken the tournament to new heights. Platforms like March Madness Live, CBS Sports, and the NCAA's own website and app allow fans to watch games on demand, stream from their phones or tablets, and receive real-time updates and highlights. Social media platforms like Twitter, Instagram, and TikTok amplify this reach, offering instant replays, memes, and fan reactions. These digital tools make March Madness not just a televised event, but a fully interactive experience, accessible anytime and anywhere.

Broadcasting has also played a key role in shaping the narrative of the tournament. Iconic announcers like Jim Nantz, Verne Lundquist, and Gus Johnson have given voice to unforgettable moments, embedding them into sports lore with lines that live on long after the games end. Sideline reporters, studio analysts, and pre- and post-game coverage bring added depth, giving fans insights into player stories, coaching strategies, and historical context.

In this chapter, we'll examine the evolution of March Madness broadcasting—from radio waves to 5G streaming—highlighting how media partnerships, technology, and storytelling have turned the NCAA Tournament into a cultural juggernaut. The madness, after all, isn't just played—it's broadcast to the world, shaping how we remember every shot, shock, and shining moment.

The Business of Broadcasting

The NCAA Men's Basketball Tournament is more than just a sporting spectacle—it is a massive commercial enterprise, and at the heart of its financial engine lies the business of broadcasting. From billion-dollar media rights deals to advertising revenue and digital monetization, the broadcasting side of March Madness has transformed the tournament into one of the most lucrative and influential properties in the world of sports.

The cornerstone of this broadcasting empire is the TV rights deal between the NCAA and the joint venture of CBS Sports and Turner Sports (Warner Bros. Discovery). In 2010, the NCAA signed a groundbreaking 14-year, $10.8 billion agreement to televise every game of the men's tournament. This deal was extended in 2016 for an additional $8.8 billion, bringing the total value to over $19.6 billion through 2032. This long-term partnership ensures that every game is broadcast live on CBS, TBS, TNT, or truTV, giving fans full access to the tournament from the First Four to the Final Four.

This arrangement provides significant revenue to the NCAA, which distributes the majority of it back to Division I schools through the "Basketball Performance Fund" and other support programs. The financial windfall enables schools to fund athletic departments, invest in facilities, and support non-revenue sports. The broadcasting revenue also underscores the growing importance of media in shaping collegiate athletics, as TV money now plays a central role in conference realignment and institutional strategy.

One of the biggest beneficiaries of the business of broadcasting is advertising. March Madness is a magnet for advertisers, attracting tens of millions of viewers and creating a captive audience over three weeks. In 2023 alone, advertising revenue for the tournament surpassed $1 billion, according to research firm Kantar. Major brands such as Capital One, AT&T, and Coca-Cola anchor their marketing campaigns around March Madness, often rolling out custom commercials, sponsorships, and digital campaigns.

The tournament's format also plays perfectly into the needs of broadcasters and advertisers. With dozens of games spread across multiple channels over several days, networks can offer a high volume of commercial slots while keeping engagement levels high. The event's high stakes and unpredictable outcomes keep viewers glued to their screens, minimizing channel switching and maximizing ad exposure.

In addition to traditional TV, digital broadcasting has become a major component of the business. Platforms like March Madness Live offer streaming access to all games with multiple camera angles, live stats, and real-time brackets. These platforms monetize through a mix of subscription authentication, pre-roll and in-game ads, and sponsorships. As younger audiences migrate to mobile and digital viewing, the NCAA and its broadcasting partners are investing heavily in interactive content and second-screen experiences to maintain relevance.

The business of broadcasting March Madness is not just about showing games—it's about owning the cultural moment. Through expertly crafted narratives, prime-time exposure, and multi-platform distribution, broadcasters have turned the NCAA Tournament into a media juggernaut. It's a powerful reminder that behind every buzzer-beater lies a carefully orchestrated and highly profitable broadcast machine.

How TV and Streaming Changed the Game

The rise of television and streaming has completely transformed how the NCAA Men's Basketball Tournament—better known as March Madness—is experienced, consumed, and remembered. Once limited to local radio broadcasts and newspaper box scores, the tournament is now a global media event, available on demand across multiple screens, platforms, and time zones. This evolution has not only expanded the reach of the tournament but has also reshaped its impact on fans, players, broadcasters, and the game itself.

In the early days, coverage of the tournament was minimal. Before the 1980s, only a handful of games were televised, often limited to regional interest or the Final Four. It wasn't until CBS acquired exclusive broadcasting rights in 1982 that the tournament began receiving full national exposure. The network saw the potential in March Madness as a dramatic, narrative-driven sporting event and invested heavily in turning it into must-see TV. With compelling storylines, underdog runs, and last-second heroics, CBS transformed the tournament into a national obsession.

The biggest shift came in 2010, when the NCAA partnered with CBS and Turner Sports (TBS, TNT, and truTV) in a landmark media rights deal. This agreement ensured that every single game of the tournament would be televised live, a first in American sports history. No longer did fans have to wait for highlights or limited coverage—they could now watch every matchup in real time, regardless of location or seeding. This decision expanded the tournament's accessibility and significantly increased fan engagement.

Streaming technology has taken this accessibility to a new level. With platforms like March Madness Live, fans can now watch games on smartphones, tablets, laptops, and smart TVs. These apps offer more than just live games—they include real-time stats, alternate camera angles, interactive brackets, and social media integration. Viewers no longer have to choose one game at a time; they can follow multiple matchups simultaneously, switching between close contests and upset alerts with just a few taps.

This digital transformation has also changed the way fans interact with the tournament. Social media platforms like Twitter, Instagram, and TikTok have become integral parts of the viewing experience, allowing fans to share reactions, follow commentary, and participate in memes and debates in real time. Streaming and social media have turned March Madness from a passive viewing experience into an active, communal one.

For players and programs, the impact has been equally significant. Exposure through national TV and streaming can elevate the profile of mid-major schools, help players build personal brands, and increase recruiting visibility. A standout performance in a single game can go viral, earning a player national recognition and even future endorsement opportunities, especially in the NIL era.

Finally, the widespread coverage has also influenced the style of play. With every game now under national scrutiny, coaches and players are more aware of their platform. There's a stronger emphasis on pace, excitement, and high-level execution, as every play has the potential to become a defining moment on the national stage.

In short, TV and streaming haven't just enhanced the way we watch March Madness—they've redefined it. What was once a niche tournament is now a 24/7 multimedia experience, deeply woven into the fabric of sports culture.

Iconic Commentators and Memorable Calls

The NCAA Men's Basketball Tournament is not only remembered for the buzzer-beaters, Cinderella stories, and championship glory—it's also etched in the collective memory through the voices that brought those moments to life. Iconic commentators and their memorable calls have become a defining part of March Madness, elevating dramatic plays into timeless moments and helping shape the emotional resonance of the tournament. The voices behind the madness—filled with energy, shock, passion, and poetic timing—are just as unforgettable as the action on the court.

At the top of the list is Jim Nantz, the longtime lead play-by-play announcer for CBS Sports, whose smooth, composed delivery has become synonymous with Final Fours and championship games. Since taking over the role in 1991, Nantz has called some of the most historic moments in tournament history, from buzzer-beaters to emotional finales. His famous line, "And the slipper still fits!" during Gonzaga's 1999 Cinderella run, captured the nation's imagination and added to the mythology of the mid-major's magical journey.

Another legend in the March Madness booth is Verne Lundquist, whose warmth and enthusiasm made him a fan favorite. His call of Christian Laettner's iconic game-winning shot in 1992—"Yes! And the Blue Devils win it!"—still gives fans chills. Lundquist had a unique ability to blend joy, tension, and surprise into his calls, creating an authentic connection with viewers. His retirement from NCAA Tournament coverage in 2016 marked the end of an era, but his voice remains forever linked to some of the tournament's greatest highlights.

Gus Johnson, known for his unfiltered passion and high-octane delivery, brought a different kind of energy to March Madness.

Whether it was a deep three-pointer, a wild comeback, or a stunning upset, Johnson's explosive reactions matched the madness unfolding on the court. His call of UCLA's miraculous comeback against Gonzaga in 2006—"Heart! Break! City!"—perfectly encapsulated the chaos and emotion that defines the tournament. Fans often associate Johnson with the most thrilling finishes, and his voice has become a symbol of March's unpredictability.

Bill Raftery, a former coach turned color commentator, has added depth, humor, and signature phrases to broadcasts for decades. Known for his enthusiastic "Onions!" after clutch shots and "With a kiss!" on soft banked layups, Raftery brings personality and insight to every game. His chemistry with Jim Nantz and Grant Hill in recent Final Fours has kept the broadcasts lively, informative, and memorable.

These commentators do more than describe the action—they create lasting emotional connections. Their voices turn great plays into iconic memories. Whether it's the stunned silence that follows a major upset, the rising pitch of a game-winning three, or the final words as a champion is crowned, these calls live on in highlight reels, documentaries, and fans' hearts.

In the story of March Madness, the players make the plays—but the commentators give them life. Their words echo long after the games end, forever tying their voices to the moments that define college basketball's greatest stage.

Behind the Scenes of a National Telecast

While millions of fans tune in to watch the NCAA Men's Basketball Tournament from the comfort of their homes, few fully grasp the complex and meticulously coordinated effort that goes into producing a national telecast of a March Madness game. Behind the scenes, an army of producers, directors, camera operators, engineers, graphics teams, statisticians, and support staff work together to deliver a seamless, high-quality broadcast experience. Each game is more than just basketball—it's a live production on a grand scale, requiring precision, planning, and real-time decision-making.

It all begins weeks in advance with logistical preparation. Once the tournament bracket is set, broadcast teams assigned to each venue coordinate with the NCAA, host universities, and arena staff to plan the technical setup. Multiple production trucks are stationed outside the arena, each functioning as a mobile control room. These trucks house the director, technical director, audio engineers, replay operators, and graphics teams. Inside, every second of the telecast is managed, from camera angles and instant replays to commentator audio levels and commercial breaks.

Camera coverage is a central component. A typical March Madness game uses 10–15 cameras positioned strategically around the court: baseline, sideline, overhead, and handheld. These include slow-motion cameras, robotic cams, and overhead "spidercams" to capture dynamic, cinematic shots. Each camera is controlled by a trained operator who communicates with the director via headset. The director calls the shots in real time, selecting which angles make it to the screen, often within milliseconds of the action.

The broadcast team also includes a producer who manages the pacing of the show, ensuring proper transitions between live play, replays, commentator discussions, and on-screen graphics. They work closely with graphics operators to provide real-time stats, player bios, shot charts, and score updates. Every graphic that appears on screen is pre-programmed and triggered at the right moment to keep viewers informed and engaged without overwhelming them.

Meanwhile, audio engineers balance multiple sound feeds: court microphones, crowd noise, commentator headsets, and background music. Their goal is to create an immersive atmosphere—where fans at home can hear the squeak of sneakers, the roar of the crowd, and the tension in the announcers' voices without any one element overpowering the others.

Commentators and analysts receive real-time updates from spotters and statisticians in the booth, who track fouls, substitutions, and milestones as they happen. Sideline reporters, meanwhile, coordinate with producers to deliver timely injury updates, coach interviews, and human-interest stories—adding depth to the broadcast.

During commercial breaks, the control room switches to pre-planned ad packages, often with seconds to spare. Timing is critical; games must return from break just before inbound plays, and national sponsors expect precise ad placement.

In total, a single March Madness game broadcast involves over 50 professionals, all working in unison to deliver a polished product. The coordination, technology, and creativity behind the scenes are what make each game feel so fluid and immersive.

While the spotlight shines on the players and coaches, the magic of March Madness is made possible by the tireless work of the broadcast team—telling the story, capturing the emotion, and turning live basketball into an unforgettable viewing experience.

Chapter 10
Legacy and Looking Ahead

As the final buzzer sounds and confetti falls on the newly crowned national champions, the NCAA Men's Basketball Tournament leaves behind more than just a trophy presentation—it leaves a lasting legacy. March Madness is more than a sporting event; it's a cultural institution, an economic force, and a yearly tradition that brings together generations of fans, athletes, and institutions. Over the decades, the tournament has shaped the way we experience college sports, defined careers, sparked national conversations, and created some of the most iconic moments in athletic history.

Chapter 10 explores the legacy of March Madness—what it has meant to the game of basketball, to American sports culture, and to those who participate in it, from players and coaches to broadcasters, fans, and universities. The tournament has elevated schools into national prominence, turned athletes into legends overnight, and given mid-major programs a platform to dream big and compete with giants. From Magic Johnson and Larry Bird's epic 1979 title clash to buzzer-beaters, bracket busters, and Cinderella runs that captured the nation's imagination, March Madness has carved a permanent place in our collective memory.

But this chapter also looks forward, examining how the tournament is continuing to evolve in an era of rapid change. With the advent of Name, Image, and Likeness (NIL) deals, the explosion of digital media, and shifts in athlete mobility through the transfer portal, the landscape of college basketball is in flux. Questions about amateurism, student-athlete rights, competitive balance, and conference realignment are reshaping the sport from the ground up. And yet, despite all this transformation, March Madness remains a resilient institution—capable of adapting while preserving the chaos, excitement, and emotion that make it special.

Looking ahead, the tournament faces both opportunities and challenges. On one hand, new technologies promise to enhance the fan experience through augmented reality, real-time analytics, and more personalized content. Global interest in basketball is growing, offering the potential for March Madness to extend its reach far beyond American borders. On the other hand, the pressures of commercialization, athlete compensation, and media fragmentation present questions about how the tournament will maintain its integrity and appeal.

One of the most enduring aspects of March Madness is its ability to create lasting memories and legacy moments. It's not just about who wins—it's about how they win, what obstacles they overcome, and the stories they write along the way. The tournament has become a rite of passage for players and fans alike, a celebration of sport at its most unpredictable and emotionally rich.

In this final chapter, we'll reflect on how March Madness became what it is today, how it continues to influence lives and institutions, and how it must evolve to stay relevant in the years to come. Whether you're filling out your first bracket or your fiftieth, March Madness remains a symbol of hope, heartbreak, triumph, and the timeless thrill of competition. Its legacy is still being written—and the madness shows no signs of slowing down.

Most Memorable Tournaments

Over the decades, the NCAA Men's Basketball Tournament has produced countless unforgettable moments, but some tournaments stand out as especially iconic for the drama they delivered, the legacies they shaped, and the way they captured the imagination of fans across the nation. These are the tournaments that transformed players into legends, turned underdogs into household names, and reminded everyone why March Madness is among the most thrilling spectacles in all of sports.

The 1983 tournament remains one of the most improbable and heartwarming stories in college basketball history. NC State, a 6-seed coached by the energetic and inspirational Jim Valvano, barely made it into the tournament but managed to claw their way through the bracket with a series of last-minute victories. Their championship game against Houston's "Phi Slama Jama" team, featuring future NBA Hall of Famers Hakeem Olajuwon and Clyde Drexler, ended with one of the most iconic plays in tournament history—a last-second dunk by Lorenzo Charles that secured a 54–52 victory and set off a jubilant celebration. Valvano's search for someone to hug as he ran across the court became a defining image of March Madness.

Another unforgettable tournament came in 1992, when Duke and Kentucky squared off in what is widely regarded as the greatest game ever played in NCAA Tournament history. The Elite Eight matchup was a back-and-forth battle that culminated in Christian Laettner's miracle turnaround jumper at the buzzer after a full-court pass from Grant Hill. The shot not only sent Duke to the Final Four, but it also etched Laettner's name into college basketball folklore. Duke would go on to win the championship, but the memory of that single shot remains one of the most celebrated moments in tournament history.

In 2006, the magic of March reached new heights with George Mason University's Cinderella run. As an 11-seed from the Colonial Athletic Association, George Mason stunned the basketball world by defeating Michigan State, North Carolina, and Connecticut—three storied programs—on their way to the Final Four. Their improbable journey captivated the nation and reaffirmed the idea that anything is possible in March, giving mid-major programs across the country a renewed sense of belief.

The 2008 tournament was memorable for a different reason: for the first time ever, all four No. 1 seeds reached the Final Four. Kansas, North Carolina, UCLA, and Memphis collided in a showdown of basketball royalty. The championship game between Kansas and Memphis provided one of the most thrilling finishes in tournament history. With seconds remaining and Kansas trailing, Mario Chalmers hit a game-tying three-pointer that sent the contest into overtime, where the Jayhawks would eventually secure the title. The level of play throughout the tournament and its epic conclusion made 2008 one of the most celebrated years in NCAA history.

And then came 2018, when UMBC (University of Maryland, Baltimore County) pulled off the unthinkable: as a 16-seed, they defeated No. 1 overall seed Virginia in dominating fashion, 74–54. It marked the first time in tournament history that a 16-seed had defeated a 1-seed, shattering expectations and reminding fans that no team is safe in March. It was more than a win—it was a moment that redefined the possible.

These tournaments live on not just for the games, but for the emotion, the chaos, and the unforgettable stories they gave to the world of college basketball. They are the reason we watch, why we believe, and why March Madness continues to captivate year after year.

Future Trends in Men's College Basketball

As college basketball continues to evolve, several emerging trends are reshaping the landscape of the men's game—both on and off the court. Driven by technological innovation, policy changes, and shifting cultural expectations, these developments are influencing how programs recruit, how players train and compete, and how fans engage with the sport. While tradition remains a strong pillar of the NCAA Tournament, the future of men's college basketball is being defined by adaptability, modernization, and a rapidly changing environment.

One of the most significant trends is the continued expansion and normalization of Name, Image, and Likeness (NIL) rights. Since being introduced in 2021, NIL has empowered student-athletes to earn compensation through endorsements, sponsorships, merchandise sales, and social media influence. As NIL markets mature, schools are investing in branding education, marketing support, and partnerships with agencies to help players navigate these new opportunities. This has transformed recruiting, with players considering not just basketball fit, but also the financial and promotional advantages of joining a particular program. NIL will continue to influence where players choose to play, how long they stay, and how schools compete for top talent.

Closely connected is the rise of the transfer portal, which has made player movement more fluid than ever before. With fewer restrictions on transferring and no requirement to sit out a year after a first transfer, athletes now have greater freedom to find the right program, system, or personal situation. Coaches must now re-recruit their own rosters each year while also scouting the portal for experienced players who can make an immediate impact. The portal has effectively created a new recruiting season, and it's reshaping how teams build continuity and chemistry.

On the court, analytics and technology are becoming central to strategy and player development. Coaching staffs increasingly rely on advanced data to make decisions about rotations, matchups, pace, shot selection, and defensive schemes. Wearable tech and motion tracking allow for more precise training regimens, workload management, and injury prevention. As the sport becomes more data-driven, teams with access to high-level analytics and personnel are gaining a competitive edge.

Another major shift is the continued emphasis on versatility and positionless play. The future of the game favors players who can shoot, handle, defend, and switch across multiple positions. Big men are developing perimeter skills, and guards are expected to rebound and defend in the post. This trend is pushing college programs to focus more on player development and adaptability than traditional roles or size-based lineups.

The globalization of recruiting is also accelerating. With basketball's popularity expanding internationally, more college programs are recruiting outside the U.S. for talent. International players bring diverse styles and skill sets, and some schools are building pipelines to countries like Canada, Australia, and various parts of Europe and Africa. This broader talent pool adds new dynamics to rosters and elevates the overall quality of the college game.

Finally, fan engagement is evolving through digital media, streaming, and interactive content. From real-time stats to social media reactions, fans now expect a more immersive and personalized experience. Schools and broadcasters are adapting by integrating behind-the-scenes access, augmented reality, and influencer marketing into their outreach.

In the coming years, these trends will continue to reshape men's college basketball, ensuring that while the madness of March remains, it will do so in a faster, smarter, and more connected world.

Will the Format Change?

The NCAA Men's Basketball Tournament has long been revered for its iconic format—68 teams, single elimination, and three thrilling weeks of win-or-go-home drama. It's a structure that has stood the test of time and captured the imagination of sports fans across generations. But as the landscape of college athletics continues to shift due to realignment, expanding conferences, media contracts, and the evolving needs of student-athletes, the question is becoming more relevant than ever: Will the format change?

For now, the 68-team format remains firmly in place. Introduced in 2011 with the addition of the "First Four" play-in games, the current setup allows for inclusivity across conferences while preserving the traditional 64-team bracket that fans know and love. The format strikes a delicate balance—giving smaller conferences a chance at representation while rewarding power programs with higher seeding and favorable matchups. It creates space for Cinderella stories without diluting the competitive rigor of the tournament. In this way, the NCAA has been hesitant to tamper with a product that works exceptionally well from both competitive and commercial standpoints.

However, pressure to expand further has grown in recent years. With conference realignment reshaping the college sports landscape and the Power Five conferences consolidating more elite teams, there are increasing calls to widen the tournament field. Proponents of expansion argue that as more quality programs are squeezed into the same limited number of at-large spots, the current format risks excluding deserving teams, especially those in stronger conferences who play grueling schedules. Some suggest that expanding to 72 or even 96 teams could address this, though opponents fear it would water down the quality of competition and disrupt the magic of the opening weekend.

Another possible change concerns automatic bids. Currently, every conference tournament winner earns an automatic spot in the field, regardless of their regular season performance. With growing financial stakes and competitive imbalance between high-major and mid-major conferences, there have been whispers—especially from power schools—about reconsidering how those automatic bids are awarded. While it remains unlikely in the short term, such a move would fundamentally change the democratic spirit of March Madness, which is built on the idea that anyone can make a run, regardless of size or prestige.

Technological advances could also drive changes in how the format is executed, if not how it's structured. Concepts like live reseeding after each round, more neutral-site games in the early rounds, or regional realignment based on seeding fairness have all been floated as ways to make the tournament more equitable or logistically efficient. While none of these ideas have gained formal traction, they reflect the broader discussion about optimizing the fan and team experience.

In the end, the magic of March Madness lies in its structure—every game matters, every team has a shot, and the unpredictable nature of the bracket is part of what makes it so beloved. Any change to the format would need to preserve that magic. While minor tweaks may come, a major overhaul remains unlikely—at least for now. Still, in the ever-changing world of college athletics, even the most sacred traditions are never entirely off the table.

Why March Madness Will Always Matter

March Madness holds a unique place in the sports world—an annual celebration of unpredictability, passion, and pure competition. While the landscape of college athletics continues to evolve through NIL deals, conference realignment, and technological disruption, the NCAA Men's Basketball Tournament retains a cultural power that few other sporting events can match. March Madness will always matter because it represents more than just a basketball tournament—it embodies tradition, opportunity, and the collective spirit of fans across generations.

One of the reasons March Madness remains vital is its democratic nature. In a world where professional sports are often dominated by money, contracts, and dynasties, the NCAA Tournament offers a level playing field. Any team, from any conference, has a chance to dance. Programs from small schools with modest budgets go head-to-head with national powerhouses, and every year, at least one of them proves they belong. These Cinderella stories fuel the essence of the tournament, giving hope to underdogs and inspiring fans who love the idea that anything is possible.

The single-elimination format adds to the gravity and urgency of every game. There are no do-overs, no series, no time to recalibrate. One cold shooting night, one clutch buzzer-beater, one incredible performance can change the fate of a team's season. This high-stakes structure ensures that every moment counts, creating emotional peaks and valleys that no other American sporting event replicates over such a short time span. The drama is authentic, the pressure palpable, and the reactions—from tears to triumph—entirely human.

March Madness also thrives because it is shared by the many, not just the few. The bracket itself turns millions of people into active participants, regardless of how closely they follow college basketball. Office pools, family competitions, and friendly rivalries bring people together in ways that transcend geography or allegiance. People who couldn't name a single player before March suddenly become invested in the outcomes of teams they've never watched, because their bracket depends on it. This collective participation builds a nationwide sense of community and excitement that few events can replicate.

The tournament has also proven incredibly adaptable, embracing change while preserving its core. Games are now available on every screen, social media amplifies every highlight, and new generations of fans can follow the madness from anywhere in the world. The NCAA, broadcasters, and sponsors have skillfully kept March Madness relevant without compromising what makes it special: competitive balance, storytelling, and unpredictability.

Moreover, for the players and coaches, the tournament remains a proving ground. One great run can define a career, open doors to the NBA, or bring national attention to a once-overlooked school. It's where names are made and legacies born. Players leave their mark not just through statistics, but through unforgettable moments that live on in highlight reels and collective memory.

Ultimately, March Madness will always matter because it taps into something universal—hope, heart, and the thrill of the unexpected. As long as people believe in the power of dreams, and as long as the game is played with passion and pride, the madness of March will never lose its magic.

Chapter 11
Women in the Madness

For decades, the NCAA Men's Basketball Tournament—March Madness—has been celebrated as a pinnacle of athletic competition, drama, and national unity. Yet, for much of its storied history, the voices, contributions, and presence of women in and around the tournament have been limited or overlooked. That narrative, however, is changing. Chapter 11: Women in the Madness explores the growing and vital role that women play in the world of men's college basketball, from the broadcast booth and analyst desk to the production truck, the coaching sidelines, and the executive offices shaping the tournament's future.

Historically, men's sports—especially those with massive national audiences like March Madness—have been dominated by male perspectives. Broadcast crews, commentators, analysts, and even behind-the-scenes producers were almost exclusively men for many years. But over the past two decades, women have steadily broken into these spaces, not as tokens, but as experts, leaders, and innovators. This evolution hasn't just diversified who tells the story of the tournament; it's elevated the depth and quality of the coverage, bringing new insights, experiences, and voices to a stage that commands the attention of millions.

The presence of female broadcasters and analysts in men's basketball coverage has become increasingly visible and respected. Pioneers like Doris Burke, who began as a sideline reporter and eventually became the first woman to call a nationally televised NBA game, opened doors for others to follow in both the men's and women's games. Today, female voices offer sharp analysis, historical perspective, and a passion for the game that resonates with a diverse and growing audience. Their rise reflects a shift in both public perception and institutional openness to inclusion at the highest levels of sports media.

Women are also making an impact behind the cameras, where decisions about narrative, tone, and visual storytelling are made. From directors and producers to statisticians and camera operators, women are increasingly occupying roles that shape how the tournament is seen and experienced. Their work ensures that the portrayal of March Madness reflects a broader and more inclusive reality—one that speaks not only to die-hard fans but to new generations of viewers who expect representation and authenticity in what they consume.

Coaching and administrative roles are seeing slow but meaningful progress as well. Women are being hired into support and operations roles within men's basketball programs, and some have risen into assistant coaching and player development positions—once thought to be unattainable in the male-dominated coaching hierarchy. Additionally, female athletic directors and NCAA executives now help shape the rules, policies, and strategic vision that guide the tournament's future.

This chapter will spotlight these developments and the individuals leading the charge. From breaking barriers to setting new standards, women are reshaping what it means to be part of March Madness. Their inclusion is not just a step toward equality—it's an evolution that enriches the tournament, broadens its reach, and ensures that the madness is truly for everyone.

Breaking Barriers: The History of Women in Men's College Basketball Broadcasting

The world of men's college basketball broadcasting has long been dominated by male voices, both in front of and behind the camera. For decades, the narrative of March Madness was shaped by men—announcing the games, analyzing the plays, and directing the camera angles. However, the tide began to turn as determined and talented women pushed through cultural and institutional barriers to earn their place in this highly competitive field. The history of women in men's college basketball broadcasting is one of persistence, progress, and pioneering change that continues to evolve to this day.

In the early years of NCAA Tournament coverage, there were virtually no women in the broadcast booth or on the production team. Women who aspired to work in sports media were often relegated to roles in less prominent sports or behind-the-scenes administrative tasks. But in the 1970s and 1980s, as the broader women's rights movement gained momentum and Title IX began to reshape college athletics, a new generation of female journalists and broadcasters began to emerge—eager to break into the male-dominated world of sports.

One of the trailblazers was Lesley Visser, who made history as the first female NFL beat writer and later became a familiar face in NCAA Tournament coverage. In 1990, she became the first woman to serve as a sideline reporter during the men's NCAA Final Four for CBS. Her presence, professionalism, and deep knowledge of the game opened the door for other women to enter the field with credibility and confidence. Visser's career demonstrated that women could not only cover men's sports with authority but also contribute meaningfully to the storytelling that surrounds major athletic events.

In the years that followed, other pioneering women like Andrea Joyce, Tracy Wolfson, and Allie LaForce became fixtures in March Madness coverage. As sideline reporters, they provided real-time injury updates, emotional post-game interviews, and insights that enriched the viewing experience. Their work helped bridge the gap between the court and the audience, offering access and depth that went beyond the play-by-play.

The real turning point came when women began to enter the analyst and play-by-play roles, traditionally reserved for former male players and coaches. Doris Burke, though more commonly associated with the NBA, became a symbol of this shift. Her deep basketball IQ, calm presence, and analytical insight won over skeptics and set a new standard for female commentators. Others like Debbie Antonelli brought decades of basketball experience to men's tournament broadcasts, offering perspective with authority and enthusiasm.

Behind the scenes, more women have also risen through the ranks in production, directing, editing, and technical roles. They play critical parts in shaping how the tournament is presented—from camera work and graphics to editorial decisions and highlight reels. Their growing presence reflects a broader shift in the industry toward inclusion and diversity.

Today, women are not only participating in March Madness broadcasts—they are helping define them. The history of women in men's college basketball broadcasting is still being written, but it's clear that the days of a single voice are over. The modern sound of March now includes a powerful, diverse chorus—one that reflects the true spirit of the game.

Female Analysts and Their Rising Influence on Tournament Coverage

In recent years, female analysts have emerged as some of the most compelling and insightful voices in men's college basketball coverage, reshaping the way audiences engage with March Madness. While women have long contributed behind the scenes or as sideline reporters, their transition into roles traditionally dominated by former male players and coaches marks a significant shift in the broadcasting landscape. Female analysts are no longer just present — they are now shaping narratives, influencing opinions, and bringing new depth to tournament coverage.

At the forefront of this movement is Debbie Antonelli, one of the most respected voices in college basketball broadcasting. A former player at NC State and a longtime analyst across ESPN, CBS, and Turner Sports, Antonelli has covered both men's and women's tournaments with precision and poise. Her basketball acumen, preparation, and ability to break down complex plays have earned her widespread respect — not just among fans, but also from coaches, players, and her peers in the industry. She brings a coach's mind to the analyst desk, offering strategic insights on matchups, adjustments, and team dynamics that rival any analyst in the game.

The influence of female analysts also stems from the unique perspectives they bring to the commentary booth. Their ability to see the game differently — often with an eye toward fundamentals, team chemistry, and decision-making under pressure — adds richness to the broadcast. Unlike some former players who focus heavily on physicality or highlight-reel moments, many female analysts emphasize game flow, mental toughness, and coaching nuances. This analytical diversity makes the coverage more comprehensive and educational for fans.

Female voices in the analyst chair also represent a broader cultural shift in sports media. Networks and audiences are increasingly recognizing that expertise is not defined by gender. The rise of analysts like LaChina Robinson, Christy Winters-Scott, and Monica McNutt has highlighted the depth of basketball knowledge among women and expanded the talent pool for high-profile tournament coverage. These analysts have built careers on deep research, consistent performance, and the ability to connect with viewers—traits that are invaluable during high-stakes tournament games.

Their growing presence has had a tangible impact on representation and visibility. When young girls watching March Madness see knowledgeable, confident women breaking down plays, offering critical analysis, and owning the moment on national television, it reshapes what's possible. It signals that basketball media is not a boys' club—that talent, preparation, and insight can shine regardless of gender.

Moreover, the inclusion of female analysts contributes to a more inclusive viewing experience. Their presence challenges outdated assumptions about who can speak with authority in sports and invites a broader, more diverse audience to feel connected to the coverage. It also encourages richer discussions and deeper storytelling, as analysts with varied backgrounds bring different angles and personal experiences to the table.

As March Madness continues to grow in reach and significance, female analysts are not just rising—they are redefining excellence in basketball commentary. Their influence ensures that the tournament remains dynamic, modern, and reflective of the diverse world in which it exists. The analyst desk, once a space of uniform voices, is now a platform for brilliance from all corners of the game.

Trailblazing Coaches and Contributors Behind the Scenes

While much of the spotlight during March Madness is focused on players and head coaches, a powerful and often underappreciated force behind the scenes includes the growing number of trailblazing women who contribute to the success of men's college basketball in various impactful roles. From assistant coaches and player development specialists to athletic trainers, team operations managers, and front office executives, women are increasingly making their mark within programs, offering expertise, leadership, and a fresh perspective to a traditionally male-dominated sport.

One of the most groundbreaking shifts in recent years has been the inclusion of women on coaching staffs for men's teams. Though still relatively rare, this development represents a monumental cultural change in how expertise and leadership are valued. Women like Edniesha Curry, who served as an assistant coach for the University of Maine men's basketball team and later the NBA's Portland Trail Blazers, have paved the way by breaking stereotypes and earning respect through their deep knowledge of the game, player rapport, and coaching ability. Curry's presence on a men's bench was not symbolic—it was strategic. Her work focused on player development, mental preparation, and skill-building, helping male athletes reach their potential through a fresh lens.

These roles are not just limited to coaches. Team operations managers, who handle the critical logistics of travel, scheduling, and daily coordination, are increasingly being led by capable women.

Their organizational expertise ensures that teams function smoothly behind the scenes, allowing coaches and players to focus on performance. Women in these roles often serve as the connective tissue within programs, maintaining structure and consistency through the hectic pace of a collegiate season.

Athletic trainers and sports performance directors also play an essential role. Women like Amy Bragg, who made her mark in college and professional athletics, bring science-based approaches to athlete health, injury prevention, and conditioning. Their insight into recovery protocols, nutrition, and mental wellness is now considered indispensable to modern programs aiming for peak performance in the tournament. As the physical demands of the game increase, the importance of these contributors continues to rise.

Another area where women are influencing the men's game is within athletic departments and executive roles. Female athletic directors, assistant ADs, and NCAA decision-makers are increasingly involved in shaping the policies, funding priorities, and compliance structures that affect how men's basketball programs operate. Leaders like Nina King, Athletic Director at Duke University, are responsible for guiding some of the nation's most high-profile programs, demonstrating that leadership in sports administration knows no gender.

While challenges remain, especially in terms of representation and access, the presence of these trailblazing women is a sign of meaningful progress. They are reshaping the internal culture of men's college basketball—not by imitating their male counterparts, but by bringing their own unique approaches, skills, and voices to the table. Their impact may not always be captured on highlight reels, but their contributions are deeply woven into the success stories we see every

March. As more women step into these roles and thrive, the tournament becomes not just a celebration of athletic excellence but a reflection of a more inclusive and dynamic game.

The Future of Gender Inclusion in March Madness Culture

As March Madness continues to grow as both a cultural phenomenon and a business powerhouse, conversations about gender inclusion have become more prominent, urgent, and impactful. While the NCAA Men's Basketball Tournament has historically reflected a male-dominated sports culture, recent years have seen an undeniable shift toward greater visibility, participation, and leadership from women across every aspect of the event. Looking forward, the future of gender inclusion in March Madness culture is not only promising—it's essential to the tournament's evolution and long-term relevance.

One of the most important factors driving this shift is the recognition that inclusion enriches the game. Whether in broadcasting, coaching, administration, or fan engagement, women are no longer simply breaking into spaces once considered off-limits—they are reshaping them. The presence of female analysts on men's broadcasts, female coaches on men's staffs, and women in executive positions within athletic departments is no longer viewed as groundbreaking novelty, but as a natural and necessary component of a modern sports institution. This normalization is paving the way for the next generation of women to enter and succeed in these roles with fewer barriers and more support.

Media coverage and fan response have played a major role in accelerating this cultural shift. Female commentators like Doris Burke, Debbie Antonelli, and Monica McNutt have garnered wide respect for their sharp analysis and engaging presence, demonstrating that knowledge and charisma transcend gender. Social media has amplified their voices, offering platforms to connect with audiences directly, dismantle stereotypes, and foster dialogue about inclusion in real time. As fans continue to embrace diverse perspectives, networks and production companies are more willing to invest in inclusive teams—not just for social impact, but because it improves the quality of coverage.

Beyond broadcasting, there is a growing push for equity in resources, access, and opportunities for women working in men's programs. Title IX remains a legal and cultural backbone of gender equality in college sports, and while its original focus was on participation, its broader implications now extend into hiring practices, salary equity, and visibility. Schools are being held more accountable for creating environments where women can thrive, whether that means hiring female assistant coaches for men's teams or ensuring that women in sports operations, marketing, and media receive the same opportunities for advancement as their male counterparts.

Another key driver of future inclusion is education and mentorship. Universities, athletic departments, and industry organizations are creating more programs aimed at supporting women entering sports media, coaching, and administration. Mentorship initiatives pair young professionals with seasoned veterans to bridge knowledge gaps and foster confidence. These efforts are critical to sustaining progress and building a deeper bench of qualified women ready to lead in high-profile roles within the men's basketball ecosystem.

Ultimately, the future of gender inclusion in March Madness culture is not about replacing or competing with male voices—it's about expanding the conversation, elevating excellence, and ensuring that the full spectrum of talent is represented. As the tournament continues to evolve, inclusion will not be a footnote to the madness. It will be part of the main narrative—a force driving the game forward and making the spectacle richer, smarter, and more reflective of the world watching it.

Chapter 12
Madness Beyond the Court

March Madness is best known for its high-stakes games, buzzer-beaters, and Cinderella stories that unfold on the hardwood. But beyond the painted lines of the basketball court lies a vast world of impact, influence, and meaning that reaches far beyond athletics. Chapter 12: Madness Beyond the Court explores the broader dimensions of the NCAA Men's Basketball Tournament—its cultural, economic, educational, and social significance. This chapter examines how March Madness touches communities, shapes institutions, and reflects deeper values and challenges within society.

The NCAA Tournament is more than just a sports event—it's a national ritual. Offices halt for bracket talk, TVs stream games in bars, classrooms, and living rooms, and social media explodes with commentary, memes, and live reactions. The tournament becomes a shared experience, bringing together people of all backgrounds, even those who may not follow basketball year-round. The cultural immersion into March Madness speaks to the event's unique ability to unite a divided audience through competition, drama, and human connection.

Economically, March Madness is a juggernaut. Cities that host games experience a powerful boost in tourism and local spending. Hotels are booked, restaurants are filled, and local businesses thrive from the surge of fans. For universities, a deep tournament run can mean increased applications, merchandise sales, alumni donations, and overall visibility. March Madness becomes a spotlight, and for smaller schools, that spotlight can change the course of their athletic and academic programs for years to come. The financial implications of the tournament extend into media contracts, advertising deals, and broadcasting innovations—factors that are just as crucial as the action on the court.

On a more personal level, March Madness is also a platform for athlete expression and identity. In an era where players are increasingly recognized for more than their athletic talents, the tournament becomes a stage for student-athletes to share their voices, values, and stories. From messages on sneakers to interviews that go viral, March Madness often amplifies the human side of the game. Athletes speak about mental health, social justice, family, and purpose. For many, the tournament isn't just a culmination of their college career—it's a moment of personal transformation and visibility.

The event also has educational value. Beyond the obvious tie to college life, March Madness offers insights into leadership, resilience, teamwork, and pressure management. Coaches and players often become case studies in overcoming adversity and building unity. Educators and business leaders alike use examples from the tournament to teach lessons about preparation, execution, and adaptability. The narratives of underdogs and champions alike inspire those beyond the world of sports.

In this final chapter, we explore how March Madness lives and breathes outside the box score. We'll dive into the social, economic, and cultural currents that run alongside the tournament, revealing how deeply rooted it is in American life. This madness, after all, is not confined to 94 feet—it spills into the streets, institutions, conversations, and communities that surround it, year after year.

Economic Impact on Host Cities and Universities

The NCAA Men's Basketball Tournament is not only a showcase of athletic excellence—it is also an economic engine that drives significant financial activity in the cities and universities that host its games. From the First Four in Dayton to the Final Four in a rotating slate of major metropolitan areas, March Madness delivers a surge of tourism, business engagement, and institutional exposure that creates measurable benefits far beyond the court. The economic impact on host cities and universities is one of the most powerful, if sometimes underappreciated, dimensions of the tournament.

When a city is selected to host a round of the NCAA Tournament—whether it's opening weekend games or the championship event—the preparation begins months in advance. Local businesses, hotels, restaurants, and transportation services anticipate a spike in visitors. These aren't just casual tourists—they're fans traveling from across the country to support their teams, often booking accommodations for multiple nights, dining out frequently, shopping locally, and attending ancillary events surrounding the games. According to studies conducted by various sports commissions, a single tournament weekend can generate between $10 million to $25 million in direct spending for a host city.

The influx of visitors also benefits local employment and small businesses. Temporary jobs related to security, logistics, event staffing, and hospitality are created, and existing businesses often see a significant uptick in revenue. Cities that host the Final Four, in particular, enjoy national media attention, major brand sponsorship activations, and high-profile entertainment events. These moments give host cities a platform to showcase themselves to a nationwide audience—boosting tourism, encouraging future visits, and enhancing civic pride.

For universities serving as host sites or whose teams advance deep into the tournament, the impact is equally significant. Hosting a game or being in the spotlight during March Madness brings a surge in visibility that can lead to increased student applications, higher alumni engagement, and stronger donor contributions. This phenomenon, sometimes referred to as the "Flutie Effect" (named after the quarterback whose famous game-winning play was said to have increased Boston College's national profile), is especially evident among mid-major schools. A surprise Sweet 16 or Final Four run can put a university on the map for students and supporters who may not have previously considered it.

March Madness also provides an opportunity for universities to engage with their alumni base in meaningful ways. Watch parties, special events, and fundraising campaigns tied to tournament success create a sense of community and nostalgia that often translates into increased giving. For athletic departments, a successful tournament run can lead to more merchandise sales, greater brand exposure, and long-term recruitment advantages—not just in basketball but across the school's academic and extracurricular offerings.

While the NCAA retains the bulk of the tournament's media revenue, the local and institutional economic ripple effects remain powerful. The tournament brings people together, but it also brings dollars—and for the cities and schools involved, March Madness is as much an economic opportunity as it is a sporting event. It's a moment when passion meets profit, and when the madness becomes a financial win off the court.

Social Movements, Activism, and Athlete Platforms

March Madness has long been celebrated for its thrilling gameplay and underdog victories, but in recent years, it has also emerged as a powerful stage for social movements, activism, and athlete-led advocacy. As the cultural landscape evolves, so too does the role of college athletes—not just as competitors, but as influential voices capable of driving meaningful conversations and change. The NCAA Tournament, with its massive viewership and national spotlight, provides a rare platform for student-athletes to raise awareness on issues far beyond the game.

Historically, activism in college sports was limited, often suppressed by institutional expectations and fears of backlash. But the modern generation of athletes is more socially aware, digitally connected, and empowered to speak out. March Madness, with its intense media coverage and emotional visibility, has become one of the most watched platforms where athletes can amplify their voices. From wearing messages on shoes and warm-up shirts to making bold statements in interviews and social media posts, players now use the tournament stage not just to win, but to be heard.

One of the most significant catalysts for this shift was the national reckoning with racial injustice in 2020. In response to the deaths of George Floyd, Breonna Taylor, and others, athletes across all levels of sport began using their platforms to demand change. College basketball players, many of whom come from communities directly affected by these issues, were at the forefront. During the 2021 NCAA Tournament, players from various programs wore shirts bearing phrases like "Equality," "Black Lives Matter," and "We Want Change." These messages were broadcast to millions of viewers, turning games into moments of cultural reflection and solidarity.

Athletes have also used their visibility to speak out on issues directly impacting them, such as mental health, gender equality, and fair compensation. The expansion of Name, Image, and Likeness (NIL) rights was partly driven by student-athletes who used their influence to highlight the financial inequities of college sports. Many players have used press conferences and post-game interviews to discuss the pressure of high-stakes competition, opening up important conversations about emotional well-being and the psychological toll of elite performance.

Social media has further empowered athletes to bypass traditional media gatekeepers and speak directly to fans and followers. Platforms like Twitter, Instagram, and TikTok allow players to share personal stories, highlight causes, and organize support for initiatives they care about. These digital platforms, combined with the real-time buzz of March Madness, have turned moments of activism into viral movements—ones that often gain traction far beyond the tournament itself.

Universities, too, are beginning to recognize the value of supporting their athletes' voices. Some programs have introduced initiatives focused on social responsibility, leadership training, and civic engagement. These efforts signal a growing acknowledgment that athletes are not just students or performers—they are young leaders with the power to shape public discourse.

As March Madness continues to evolve, so does its cultural role. The tournament will always be about the game, but it is increasingly about the people behind the jerseys—and the causes they champion. In the age of athlete empowerment, the madness isn't just in the brackets—it's in the boldness to stand up, speak out, and spark change.

Cultural References: Music, Memes, and Madness in Pop Culture

March Madness is more than a basketball tournament—it's a cultural phenomenon that infiltrates music, memes, fashion, and social media every spring. As millions of fans tune in to the NCAA Men's Basketball Tournament, the event transcends sports and becomes a part of the broader pop culture landscape. The excitement, unpredictability, and community of March Madness create fertile ground for artistic expression, humor, and shared experiences, making it a recurring cultural touchstone that inspires everything from viral content to chart-topping music.

Music has always played a central role in shaping the emotional tone of March Madness. The most iconic example is CBS's "One Shining Moment," a highlight montage played after the national championship game. First aired in 1987, the song has become a cherished tradition, evoking tears and chills as it captures the triumphs, heartbreaks, and unforgettable plays of the tournament. Its lyrics and melody are now embedded in the memory of fans, players, and coaches alike, marking the emotional culmination of weeks of drama and competition.

Beyond traditional broadcasts, popular music frequently intersects with the tournament in player introductions, locker room celebrations, and social media clips. Teams create hype videos featuring contemporary hip-hop and pop tracks, and championship celebrations often go viral, soundtracked by trending songs. Players themselves contribute to the musical culture—some release their own tracks or share curated playlists that reflect the mood and energy of March. This merging of music and sport strengthens the emotional connection fans have to the tournament, making it more than just a series of games.

At the same time, memes and internet culture have become inseparable from the modern March Madness experience. Social media platforms like Twitter, Instagram, TikTok, and Reddit light up with humorous takes on upsets, player reactions, and coach expressions. A dramatic facial expression, a surprising upset, or an emotional fan moment can be turned into a meme within minutes, spreading rapidly through online communities. These digital artifacts serve as a form of commentary, allowing fans to process the chaos of the tournament with humor, irony, and creativity.

Certain meme-worthy moments have even gone down in internet history—such as crying fans, improbable mascot dances, or coaches' bewildered reactions to a wild play. These moments help make the tournament accessible to even casual or non-sports fans, who may engage with the madness through entertainment rather than athletic devotion. March Madness has essentially become a shared cultural canvas, where everyone—from diehard fans to social media influencers—can contribute to the conversation.

Fashion and pop culture also blend into the madness. Custom sneakers, warm-up gear with slogans or social messages, and team-specific merchandise often reflect broader trends in streetwear and youth culture. Players with standout performances or big personalities sometimes achieve short-lived celebrity status, inspiring everything from memes to endorsements.

In sum, March Madness thrives not only in sports arenas but across pop culture platforms. Its influence extends to music, humor, fashion, and internet culture—capturing the imagination of a diverse audience. The tournament's emotional highs, dramatic turns, and sense of community make it a natural fit for cultural expression. It's not just a sporting event—it's a season of shared storytelling that touches nearly every corner of contemporary life.

Conclusion

March Madness is more than a tournament—it is a reflection of everything we love about sport, competition, and community. From its humble beginnings in 1939 to its current status as one of the most widely watched and passionately followed sporting events in the world, the NCAA Men's Basketball Tournament has transcended the boundaries of basketball to become a cultural phenomenon. It combines the intensity of competition with the unpredictability of the human spirit, delivering drama, heartbreak, joy, and redemption on an annual basis.

Throughout this book, we've explored the many dimensions of what makes March Madness so captivating. We've broken down the bracket, dissected seeding strategies, relived Cinderella runs, and celebrated the legends—both coaches and players—who left indelible marks on the tournament. We've looked at the evolution of the game itself: how rule changes, analytics, NIL policies, and the transfer portal are reshaping how college basketball operates on and off the court. We've seen how fans rally around brackets, how office pools unite coworkers, and how digital tools have turned every viewer into an engaged participant.

But the essence of March Madness goes far beyond numbers, matchups, and predictions. It's about moments. It's about the 15-seed that knocks off a 2-seed and the crowd erupts in disbelief. It's the buzzer-beater from a player whose name was unknown just a week earlier, now forever etched in highlight reels. It's the heartbreak of a missed free throw and the elation of a game-winning three. These moments become part of our collective memory, shared among generations of fans.

The tournament is also a mirror of society—reflecting our values, challenges, and progress. From gender inclusion and the rise of female voices in broadcasting, to the influence of social activism, to the celebration of diverse backgrounds and experiences, March Madness has evolved into a stage not just for basketball, but for conversation and change. Student-athletes are now more than just competitors; they are influencers, leaders, and role models using their platforms to speak out and shape the world around them.

Economically, the impact of the tournament is massive—from boosting local economies in host cities to transforming the fortunes of universities whose programs capture national attention. Culturally, it inspires music, memes, fashion, and storytelling, embedding itself in the rhythm of springtime in America. Educationally, it teaches lessons in resilience, teamwork, preparation, and pressure—lessons that apply far beyond the court.

As we look ahead, the future of March Madness will be shaped by innovation and change, yet its soul will remain intact. The format may evolve, the media landscape may shift, and players may come and go, but the spirit of the tournament—its chaos, its charm, and its community—will endure. Because March Madness is not just about basketball. It's about believing in the impossible. It's about celebrating the underdog. It's about finding magic in the madness.

And no matter what changes may come, one truth remains: every March, the nation will pause, brackets will be filled, hearts will race, and new legends will be born. The madness will always matter.

www.ingramcontent.com/pod-product-compliance
Lightning Source LLC
LaVergne TN
LVHW061552070526
838199LV00077B/7011